THE
WYOMING
BOMBER CRASH
OF
1943

Sylvia A. Bruner

SYLVIA A. BRUNER

THE
History
PRESS

Published by The History Press
An imprint of Arcadia Publishing
Charleston, SC
www.historypress.com

Copyright © 2025 by Sylvia A. Bruner
All rights reserved

First published 2025

Manufactured in the United States

ISBN 9781467158992

Library of Congress Control Number: 2025931725

Notice: The information in this book is true and complete to the best of our knowledge. It is offered without guarantee on the part of the author or The History Press. The author and The History Press disclaim all liability in connection with the use of this book.

All rights reserved. No part of this book may be reproduced or transmitted in any form whatsoever without prior written permission from the publisher except in the case of brief quotations embodied in critical articles and reviews.

Dedicated to my boys.

Illegitimi non carborundum.

CONTENTS

Foreword, by Michael Kloppenburg 7
Acknowledgements 9
Introduction 11

1. Background 13

2. William Raymond Ronaghan 18
Second Lieutenant, Pilot, 0795145

3. Anthony Joseph Tilotta 23
Second Lieutenant, Copilot, 0680767

4. Leonard Harvey Phillips 26
Second Lieutenant, Navigator, 0678761

5. Charles Hulbert Suppes III 31
Second Lieutenant, Bombardier, 0733366

6. James Alfred Hinds 34
Technical Sergeant, Aircraft Engineer/Top Turret Gunner, 39246908

7. Ferguson Theodore Bell III 37
Technical Sergeant, Radio Operator/Radio Hatch Gunner, 34334803

Contents

8. Lee Vaughan Miller 42
Sergeant, Assistant Aircraft Engineer/Waist Gunner, 35433022

9. Charles Edgar Newburn Jr. 48
Sergeant, Assistant Radio Operator/Ball Turret Gunner, 38188183

10. Jake Floyd Penick 51
Sergeant, Aircraft Gunner, 18008587

11. Lewis Marvin Shepard 54
Staff Sergeant, Assistant Aircraft Gunner, 14083794

12. Missing 67

13. Found 76

14. Recovery 79

15. Captain Kenneth Hamm 93

16. Berl Bader 105

17. Honor 111

Afterword 131
Notes 141
Bibliography 149
Index 157
About the Author 160

FOREWORD

My love for the B-17 began many years ago, when I was a child paging through a hardcover picture book of classic historical airplanes. I still have that book, and the picture remains clear in my mind's eye.

This love for the Flying Fortress intensified over the years; its clean and powerful lines remain a timeless classic for warbird enthusiasts and those who designed, built, flew and maintained these wonderful aircraft.

While searching the internet years ago, I came across a website about a B-17 crash in Wyoming. Intrigued, I read more about it. Tragically, variations of the Bomber Mountain B-17 story were often repeated as thousands of aircrewmen took to the skies in the great crusade to defeat the Axis nations. Training accidents were far too common, and many died in accidents before ever making it overseas.

Sylvia, this book's author, and I share responsibilities in running an online B-17 fan page. When she asked me to write the foreword to this book, I humbly and gratefully accepted this unique opportunity.

Years ago, I graduated from college with a bachelor's degree in history, and at one time, I wanted to teach. History, for me and many others, is magical, as past events, both personally experienced and experienced by others, beckon to us, despite the passage of time. Words and images evoke feelings, and the imaginative reader can place themselves in the context of the described events.

Preserving history and memorializing those of the past have always been important to me, and this book is a tribute to the men and women who served and their families and is a reminder of the cost of war.

—Michael Kloppenburg

ACKNOWLEDGEMENTS

I owe massive thanks to the many people who provided me with encouragement over the years, including JoAnn Mulcahy, Bill Payne, Brucie Connell, Susan Theune, Jennifer Romanoski, Kelsey McDonnell and Ken and Mary Jackman. Special thanks to the families and friends of the crew members, especially those who spent time talking and corresponding with me and who graciously allowed me to present a piece of their family's story: Nancy Bruce, Jack Shepard, Pamela Shepard, Florence Ronaghan Veale, Jim Veale, Mike Davis, Nancy and John Bair, Mike and Kathy Miller, Betsy Suppes, Wheldon and Merrice Brooks, Debra Penick McDonald, William Hinds and Glenn Newburn. I sincerely hope I have done justice in this endeavor.

Thanks also to Chuck Carrig for offering insight and assistance to this author, who does not have a military background, and to Ben Shiffer and Dave Shiffer with the Champaign Aviation Museum for identifying broken airplane parts through photographs. To Craig Cope and Karen Harvey for providing their proofreading efforts, thank you both. Particular thanks to Carina Østberg for viewing the manuscript with a discerning eye. Special thanks to Sharon Miller: I am so lucky to have received your mentorship on this project and life in general. To Gary McAulay, Ann Gallentine, Jennifer Messer, Susan Gray, Brian Rukes, Bob Nelson and the countless others at historical societies, high schools, libraries, historic sites and museums who attempted to help me track down facts or photographs, thank you for humoring me. Any mistakes or omissions are accidental and my own.

Acknowledgements

Much appreciation to all at The History Press for their guidance and assistance.

Biggest thanks to Ben, my favorite husband, who has traveled this path of historical research and hiking trips by my side while encouraging me to put this story out in the world. I could not ask for a better partner in life.

INTRODUCTION

The passing of time is a double-edged sword. As years slip away, we lose the people who were alive during the event we are researching, but also, as the years pass, records become public information or more readily available. This is one reason why historians and researchers should revisit topics that have already been explored—there may be something "new." This publication came about because many people who visit the northeast part of Wyoming and either know of or learn about the Bomber Mountain crash want to learn more. Many people have written about the crash, and many, many more have visited the site. Seeing the site firsthand is an experience that sticks in your memory. As I already possessed an interest in World War II history, this story thoroughly captured my attention when I was hired to work with the artifact collection at the Jim Gatchell Memorial Museum in Buffalo, Wyoming, in 2003. It has held my attention over the years, and there have been intermittent but persistent new facts to discover through archival and genealogical research.

Late in the night of Monday June 28, 1943

High above the earth, Billy Ronaghan felt the cold of the high-altitude summer night in his bones as he piloted the gleaming B-17 Flying Fortress over the American Northwest. The plane rattled his teeth and smelled of grease. The roaring engines drowned out all but the thoughts in his own head and the occasional radio chatter from other members of the crew. His

Introduction

crew. Billy had only known some of the men a few weeks and most of them only days, but he felt the heavy responsibility of being their pilot. He was taking them and their brand-new plane "over there." Where, exactly, over there was, well, that was still unknown. What the men on board knew for a certainty, though, was that they were destined for Europe to join the ever-increasing Allied bombing missions. With shocking speed, the German Luftwaffe was decimating aircraft and crews. To match the losses, America was frenetically churning out crews of fresh-faced boys and untested aircraft to replace the dead and downed. The European warfront needed men. They were needed in Europe.

They never made it.

1

BACKGROUND

The stories of the ten young men who died in the Bighorn Mountains of Wyoming resonate with many people. Perhaps this connection is because the fingers of World War II reached into every community and practically every home in America, whether it be through the shared trauma of losing a loved one in the conflict or simply knowing somebody who served. These men had no known connection to northeastern Wyoming prior to their deaths, but the regional community has made certain that these men are remembered in perpetuity.

Their particular aircraft now resides in pieces, both large and small, across a boulder field high in the Cloud Peak Wilderness in the Bighorn Mountains of Wyoming. There above the timberline runs a long ridgeline, now named Bomber Mountain, pointing northeast, lying southeast of Cloud Peak. The highest point of this ridge is 12,860 feet, and south of this apex rests the remains of a World War II–era B-17F bomber aircraft.

Crew member Charles Suppes wrote home about his anticipation of getting to use a new aircraft and his desire to call it *Scharazad*.[1] Most crews named World War II aircraft after they had flown together and built some camaraderie based on shared experiences, so it is unknown if this name had been accepted by the entire crew. However, given the short lifespan of this aircraft, it seems appropriate to honor Suppes's wishes to call it *Scharazad*.

Regarding individual aircraft names and artwork, Peter Bowers explains in *B-17 Flying Fortress*:

A unique practice was followed by U.S. Army heavy duty units, and to a lesser degree by medium bombers, during World War II only. It became customary for crews to either name their airplanes, paint a cartoon character or other artwork on the nose, or both. Usually, the artwork was one-sided; not duplicated on the opposite side of the nose. In a very few cases, the art was carried on the spacious vertical fin of a B-17 rather than the nose. In practice, nose art was widespread in the 8th, 12th, and 15th Air Forces in Europe and Africa and to a lesser extent on B-17s in the Pacific. In many cases, original names were transferred when a complete crew was given a replacement airplane. Also, it was inevitable that some airplane names were unknowingly duplicated.[2]

In fact, at least one other B17 was called *Scheherazade*. B-17G (serial number 42-31225) of the 447th Bomb Group was given this moniker and saw substantial action, completing 126 missions. After surviving the war, it was returned to the United States in 1945 to eventually be scrapped at Kingman, Arizona.[3]

The name Scheherazade (and a wide variety of spellings) comes from the heroine of the *1,001 Arabian Nights* stories of legend. After being betrayed by the woman he loved, the Arabian King Shahryar developed a hatred of women. He would marry a young woman each day to then have her killed that night. Scheherazade was an intelligent and creative young woman who volunteered to be his bride. She captivated the king by spinning tale after tale each night, but she never finished a story before nightfall. This kept the king occupied and therefore prevented him from taking and killing a new wife each day. Eventually, he abandoned his murderous spree completely thanks to Scheherazade's efforts.[4] Perhaps Suppes studied this ancient tale (he *was* active in his high school drama club) or had watched the 1942 movie *Arabian Nights*, in which a popular actress of the time, Maria Montez, played Scheherazade alongside actors Jon Hall, Sabu and Leif Erickson.[5] Perhaps he loved the Rimsky-Korsakov symphonic suite from 1888 called *Scheherazade*. Whatever the origins, the story and name were certainly relevant to the pop culture of the early 1940s.

The B-17 was used extensively during World War II, although it did not enter Great Britain until July 1, 1942.[6] The first bombing mission consisted of a dozen B-17Es raiding the occupied railroad marshaling yard (a "fan-shaped network of tracks and switches where railroad cars are sorted and made into trains for their respective destinations," according to *Encyclopædia Britannica*) at Rouen-Sotteville, France.[7] The statistical numbers surrounding the B-17 are staggering. With the first produced in 1935, by the end of the war, over 12,700 B-17s had been manufactured by Vega, Boeing and Douglas.[8] This mass production was due to the increased bombing missions and the heavy losses being suffered. The numbers of Army Air Corps (AAC) personnel skyrocketed; between 1942 and 1943, the number of AAC members jumped from 764,415 to 2,197,114—an increase of 187 percent.[9] These 2 million AAC personnel accounted for just over 30 percent of the U.S. Army's strength at that time. By the end of June 1943, 1,764,969 of those people were listed as being in the United States, giving an indication of the vast numbers of those in training and other services.

The number of aircraft lost within the continental United States is horrifying. In June 1943 alone, there were 41 lost (either damaged beyond repair or actually lost) in the heavy bombers category, which consisted of the B-17 and B-24.[10] From 1942 to 1945, there were 1,589 B-17 accidents in the continental United States. Of these, 284 resulted in the fatalities of 1,757 people and 479 wrecked airplanes.[11]

This F model B-17 featured over ten .50-caliber machine guns and was meant to hold a crew of ten men in the following positions: pilot, copilot, navigator, bombardier, aircraft engineer, radio operator, assistant aircraft engineer, assistant radio operator, aircraft gunner and assistant aircraft gunner. All but the pilot and copilot also had machine guns to operate in addition to manning their other positions and duties.[12] *Scharazad* featured the basic camouflage paint scheme of the day: a silver underside and olive drab green topside. The theory was that the silver would blend into the sky when viewed from below, and the green would blend into the earth when seen from above.[13]

The first order from the United States military of 599 B-17s from Douglas Aircraft came in 1942 and included *Scharazad*.[14] This facility in Long Beach, California, built 3,000 of the 12,700-plus B-17 aircraft manufactured between 1943 and 1945 for the war effort.[15] *Scharazad* was given the number 55-DL-42-3399, indicating that it was ordered for manufacture in the year 1942, was a part of production block 55 and was manufactured by Douglas in Long Beach. It was assigned a manufacturer's serial number of 8335 and cost $330,297.[16] The production block system meant that aircraft with the same block number were uniform, whether they were assembled by Boeing, Vega or Douglas. Modifications can be tracked via block information. For instance, early blocks did not include built-in bomb racks but rather featured hardware to allow racks to be installed after completion. By the time block 55 was in production, bomb racks had been integrated. Block 55 of the

Douglas production plant saw specific changes, and according to author Bill Yenne in *Building the B-17 Flying Fortress*, "In its own Block 55, which was first delivered with aircraft 42-3394 on June 2, 1943, Douglas added provisions for an auxiliary powerplant for the electrical system, a B-3 bomb release control, and an AN-5790 thermometer." It was not until the next block (60) that bombardiers would get something as basic as windshield wipers installed at their station.[17]

Like other B-17F models, 42-3399 *Scharazad* had a maximum speed of around 300 miles per hour when empty, a range of distance around 2,800 miles and a service ceiling at 37,500 feet.[18]

Scharazad was completed and delivered to the Army Air Forces on June 5, 1943 (the transition of the Army Air Corps to the Army Air Forces occurred on June 20, 1941, but there was substantial carryover of the original moniker for many months; records utilized in this publication contain both).[19] It was then ferried to the Lockheed Aircraft Modification center at Love Field, Texas, arriving on June 8 and remaining for a few weeks.[20] Manufacture centers such as the one at Long Beach were not capable of accommodating constantly changing designs and additions, so modification centers, like the one at Love Field, were often used to add variations to each aircraft. After work was completed on *Scharazad* at Love Field, it was flown to Walla Walla, Washington, on June 27. It was assigned to Pilot William Ronaghan and his crew on June 28 for their first flight. It and the crew crashed on the same day or in the early hours of June 29. *Scharazad* was removed from the AAF inventory on July 8, 1943.[21]

At the time of the crash, *Scharazad* and its crew were assigned as follows:

Station: 541st Bombardment Squadron, Pendleton Field, Oregon
Organization: 2nd Bomb, 2nd Air Force
Group: Plummer Provisional Group
Squadron: Plummer Provisional Group, Grand Island, Nebraska

This designation had not been in place for long, as crew member Lewis Shepard had written just weeks before the crash that he was in the 88th Bomber Group (H), 318th Bomb Squadron, at the Army Air Base at Walla Walla, Washington.[22] The *Scharazad* was attached to the 88th Bomb Group at Walla Walla, Washington, and was transferred to the Plummer Provisional Group operating out of the satellite base at Pendleton Field, Oregon, which was attached to the 383rd Bomb Group. The 541st Bombardment Squadron was an operational training unit from January to October 1943; the 318th

Bombardment Squadron was a replacement training unit from December 1942 to May 1944; the 383rd Bombardment Group was an operational and then replacement training unit assigned to the 2nd Air Force; and the 88th Bombardment Group was an operational and then replacement training unit assigned to the 2nd Air Force, eventually to be moved to the 3rd Air Force.[23]

The Plummer Provisional Group was in the process of moving to the 9th Heavy Bomb Processing Detachment at Grand Island, Nebraska, as detailed in a record from August 10, 1943, which reads, in part:

> *AAB Geiger Field, Wash.: Airplane with full crew was transferred from 88th Bomb Group, Walla Walla, Wash., to Plummer Provisional Group operating out of Satellite Base, Pendleton Field, Oregon, attached to 383rd Bomb Group. Plummer was in process of moving to 9th Heavy Bomb Processing Det, Grand Island, Nebraska. Plane and crew arrived at Pendleton, Oregon. Departed 28 Jun with most of the records of Plummer Provisional Group for Grand Island, Nebraska. Plane never arrived at Grand Island. Search missions have failed to locate anything. As records accompanied crew only information available is crew list.*[24]

The plane was carrying most of the records of the Plummer Provisional Group. When the *Scharazad* failed to arrive at Grand Island, there was increased confusion because the records were all onboard, with the exception of the crew list. Mary Ronaghan, the pilot's mother, wrote a letter requesting the return of William's belongings in September 1944, before the crash site had been found. She addressed the letter to the commanding officer of the 318th Squadron, 88th Bomb Group, at Walla Walla, Washington. She did this because this was William's last address she knew of, indicating the families were not up-to-date with records either.

Back to the official assignation. For people without a strong understanding of U.S. military structure, these listings often convey very little, but it does contain useful information. *Scharazad* and its crew were a part of the Plummer Provisional Group because, as the word *provisional* would imply, this group was a temporary organization used to get aircraft and men from training in the United States to the battlefront assignments where they were needed. According to a letter dated August 31, 1945, sent to Mary Ronaghan, the flight from Walla Walla, Washington, was a part of a permanent change of station, and all of the crew members' possessions were on the plane.[25]

2

WILLIAM RAYMOND RONAGHAN

Second Lieutenant, Pilot, 0795145

Born to Peter and Mary (Nilan) Ronaghan on August 15, 1918, "Billy" was the fourth of six children. Two of the Ronaghans' daughters died before reaching adulthood. Katherine died in infancy, and Margaret passed away at the age of twelve from spinal meningitis.[26] Two of their sons, Francis and James, and one daughter, Florence, all led long lives.[27] There were also a number of foster children who passed through the household, many of whom lived with the Ronaghan family until they reached adulthood and many of whom kept in touch with the family long into their adult lives. Peter Ronaghan was born and raised in Monaghan, Ireland, a small town in the border region of Ireland. He immigrated to the United States as a young man and married Mary Nilan when he was about thirty and she was twenty-three. Mary was born and raised in New York State but also had strong familial ties to Ireland, with both of her parents having been born there.[28]

During his youth, Billy worked as a carrier for the *Home News*.[29] He graduated from Evander Childs High School in the Bronx in 1936, where he had been an athletic track star. According to the high school yearbook, *The Oriole*, Billy was a member of the service league and the track squad. The quote describing him states, "Now here we have a boy who 'wants to be alone' you can find him very far from home."[30]

The Ronaghan family was civically minded, and it is no surprise that Billy served in the national guard and coast artillery and then became a New York City police officer. He enlisted in the national guard while he was still in high school and was assigned to Battery B of the 244th Coast Artillery.[31]

William Raymond Ronaghan in his New York City Police uniform. Ronaghan family collection, courtesy of the Jim Gatchell Memorial Museum.

A dedication to police service ran strong through the Ronaghan family, as Billy's father, Peter, was also a New York City police officer. Peter was an officer for many years but never found cause to fire his weapon and had a reputation of being a kind man. Billy began his services as a patrolman on June 5, 1940, in the Forty-Eighth Precinct; his shield number was 19057.[32] Because of his service in law enforcement, Billy may not have been drafted to serve in the military, as some professionals, like law enforcement officers, were considered essential on the home front. After the December 1941 attack on Pearl Harbor, however, nothing was going to prevent Billy and his brother James from military service. Their brother Francis was already in the army.

Billy enlisted in the air corps on January 23, 1942. The prior October, he had secured a letter of recommendation for his application for appointment as a flying cadet from William P. O'Brien, his captain in the 48th Precinct of the New York Police Department. In that letter, O'Brien described Billy as "upright and straightforward in character" and wrote that he was "prompt, capable and intelligent in executing all orders."[33] O'Brien's praise of Billy echoed that of Francis J. Mentzinger of Battery B, 244th Coast Artillery, New York National Guard, who, in 1937, had written a recommendation to help Billy become a New York City police officer. He also described Billy as upright and straightforward, capable and intelligent, and further noted that he had known Billy for almost two years and would "recommend him for any position he may wish to obtain."[34]

Billy Ronaghan already held a pilot's license prior to his military training, and he had purchased an Aeronca C-3 monoplane in October 1939.[35] He did well in his aviation training, reaching the rank of second lieutenant and being promoted to pilot. He received his wings upon graduating on December 13, 1942, with the class of 42-K from the George Field Army Flying School of George Field, Illinois.[36]

The youngest of the Ronaghan siblings, Florence (who went by the nickname "Babe"), was incredibly fond of her older brothers. Billy took Babe flying and kept up a steady correspondence with her and his mother once he was in the military. Florence worried about her brothers and sent them things like socks while they attended their various trainings. Billy also held his family's security and comfort close to his heart and sent money home with every paycheck he received.[37]

Military personnel records note that Billy was of lean build at six feet, one inch tall, he had brown hair and blue eyes and no known birthmarks or tattoos, his dental health was good and he was of the Catholic faith. His national guard certification lists his eye color as gray.[38]

As a pilot, Billy was responsible for his aircraft and the crew. Along with possessing a proficient understanding of flying, engine operation, flight instruments, navigation, radio operation and keeping accurate records, a pilot needed to attend to the needs of his crew, and it was up to him to foster teamwork and respect among the crew.[39]

The year 1943 was particularly difficult for the Ronaghan family, as their father, Peter, passed away that March, and Billy went missing in late June.[40] With Francis and James also being away for the war, Florence and Mary were suddenly alone after having been surrounded by the lively Ronaghan men for many years.

A regional newspaper reported:

> *Mass is Said for Safety of Missing Army Airman*
>
> *A mass for the safe return of Lieut. William Ronaghan, 1661 Lurting Ave., pilot of an Army plane missing since June 28, was said this morning at St. Francis Xavier R.C. Church, 1658 Lurting Ave.*
>
> *Ronaghan, who was a policeman attached to the Bathgate Ave. station, enlisted in the Air Force on Jan. 22, 1942. He was the first policeman at that station house, and one of the first in the entire department, to enlist.*
>
> *The pilot of a bomber, Lieut. Ronaghan was on a routine mission from Pendleton Field, Ore., when he and the other crew members disappeared.*
>
> *His father, Peter Ronaghan, who was a policeman attached to the Westchester station, died three months ago, shortly after his retirement. His son returned home to attend the services. Lieut. Ronaghan, who piloted his own plane before entering the Army, joined the Police Department on June 5, 1940.*
>
> *He has two brothers, Sgt. James Ronaghan, who is with the [Army] Air Force in this country, and Pvt. Francis Ronaghan, who is with a tank corps in Africa.*[41]

The Wyoming Bomber Crash of 1943

James, Billy and Francis Ronaghan in March 1943. *Ronaghan family collection, courtesy of the Jim Gatchell Memorial Museum.*

The memory of Billy Ronaghan was held in high regard in his community. After Billy had been missing for more than a year, the Ronaghan family's friends and neighbors still empathized with them in their frustrations and grief. On November 20, 1944, Lewis J. Valentine, police commissioner, sent the following letter.[42]

Dear Mrs. Ronaghan:

It is with deepest regret that I learn of the unfortunate news forwarded you by the United States War Department of your son, Patrolman William R. Ronaghan, serving as Second Lieutenant in the Air Corps, being presumed deceased as of June 30, 1944, due to being missing since June 28, 1943, while on flight from Pendleton Field, Oregon, to Grand Island, Nebraska.

You have the sincere sympathy of every member of this Department. We know your grief is great but you should find some consolation in knowing that your son, upholding the highest tradition of New York's Finest, did not hesitate when called upon by our loved Nation to defend its democracy.

Personally and on behalf of the members of the Police Department, City of New York, I extend to you our sincere wishes that the War Department will soon furnish you with more comforting news.

Sincerely yours,
Lewis J. Valentine, Police Commissioner

In 1946, the New York Police Department christened a police launch in Billy's honor: the *Lieutenant Ronaghan No. 1*. Billy's mother, Mary, conducted the christening and watched as the boat entered the East River for harbor patrol duty.[43]

On May 30, 2007, the New York City Police again honored Billy with the inclusion of his name and information in their Armed Forces Memorial Wall Ceremony, which was conducted with presentations by Police Commissioner Raymond W. Kelly and Mayor Michael R. Bloomberg.[44]

In 1955, Mary Ronaghan received a package from Wyoming containing Billy's dog tags. A resident of a nearby town had found them at the crash site and taken them home but eventually wanted them to be in the possession of the Ronaghan family.[45]

3

ANTHONY JOSEPH TILOTTA

Second Lieutenant, Copilot, 0680767

Tony, as friends and family called him, was born on April 5, 1919, to Santo and Vincenzia "Virginia" (Sedita) Tilotta in Houston, Texas.[46] He graduated from Sam Houston High School in 1937 and then attended Houston Vocational School. He worked as an airplane mechanic for a time at Hobby Airport in Houston before entering military services in April 1942.[47]

Tony came from a large family, having seven siblings (and another brother who passed away before he reached the age of one). His father, who went by Sam, had emigrated from Castelvetrano, Sicily, Italy, to the United States in 1902 and married Virginia in 1912. She was also from an Italian family but was born and raised in Texas as a first-generation American.[48] Santo and his brothers, Tony, Leon and Joe, all owned farmland, which they worked together.[49] Just a few months before his son Tony's death, Santo filed an application for naturalization.[50]

Tony's siblings were Phillip Raymond, Josephine Ann, Thomas Willard, Libario Louis, Louis Dan, Natalie Joann, Lee and Mary Lucille.[51] The picture of the family that emerges is one of a group of outgoing and fun-loving people. A number of

Anthony Joseph Tilotta's military portrait, showing his pilot's wings badge and officer's lapel pins. *Courtesy of the Jim Gatchell Memorial Museum.*

the brothers, including Tony, were interested in mechanics and worked on airplanes and midget race cars.[52] In the 1940 census, Virginia is listed as working as a bookkeeper at a mechanic shop. Tony grew up in the Galleria area of northwestern Houston, which was locally known as the "Onion Patch" due to the many Italian families who lived in the neighborhood.[53]

On July 26, 1941, Tony married Elsie Marie Gotcher, and they had two sons, Michael and David, although Tony never got the chance to meet David, as Elsie was pregnant with him at the time of his death.[54] Elsie would later describe Tony as quiet, courteous and very intelligent.[55] While in training, Tony attended flying school to become a pilot, graduating with class 43-E from the Blackland Army Flying School at Waco, Texas, on May 24, 1943, and receiving a promotion to second lieutenant only one month prior to his death.[56]

As the copilot, Tony needed to possess the same operational skills as the pilot so he could take command of the aircraft if such a situation arose. Although they were not held responsible for the safety and success of the crew in the same way the pilot was, copilots most certainly observed what their pilots did that was effective (or not), as they were likely to become a lead pilot/commander of their own aircraft and crew at some point during the war.[57]

Opposite: Two of Tony's brothers, Tommy (*in the car*) and Buddy, in 1940. A glimpse of life for the Tilotta family before the war. *Davis family collection.*

Right: Tony, Elsie and Michael Tilotta. Taken at their South Houston home about two weeks before Tony's death. *Davis family collection.*

Tony was buried at Woodlawn Garden of Memories in Houston, Texas, and War Department correspondence with Elsie shows that there was a holdup in acquiring a government headstone for him.[58] At the age of barely twenty, Elsie had become a widow with one small child and another on the way. Then, after two years of not knowing what had happened to her husband, she had to handle the burial of Tony's remains and navigate her way through the military process to accomplish something as simple as getting a headstone.

Tony and Elsie's son Mike was just two days shy of his first birthday when Tony died. November 1943 saw the birth of Tony and Elsie's youngest, David. In September 1948, Elsie married Chester Davis, a man who adopted both boys and provided them with the love and care of a father.[59]

4

LEONARD HARVEY PHILLIPS

Second Lieutenant, Navigator, 0678761

Leonard Phillips was born on March 29, 1921, in Omaha, Nebraska, to Libby (Moravek) and Leonard Clinton Phillips. Leonard's birth certificate notes that Leonard Sr. was from Malvern, Iowa, was twenty-three years old at the time and worked as a "collector," while Libby was from Esbon, Kansas, was twenty-four years old at the time and did housework.[60] The marriage of Libby and Leonard Sr. did not last long, and they soon divorced, with Leonard Jr. staying with his mother.[61]

When Leonard was five years old, Libby married again. The marriage took place in Big Horn County, Montana—likely in the town of Hardin, the county seat. On May 2, 1926, a thirty-year-old Dwight Josiah Fisher of Casper, Wyoming (born in Laramie, Wyoming), married Libby, who was then twenty-eight, and they both listed their residences as being in Casper. Libby's parents were listed as Anton Moravek and Frances (Matousek) Moravek, with their wedding being witnessed by Emma Marquisee and Jacob Marquisee.[62]

Like Libby, Dwight had previously been married and divorced and had a son, Dwight A. Fisher. Although Leonard seems to have had multiple half-siblings after his father, Leonard Sr., remarried, it is not clear if he knew them—or even of them. There is no public record defining what kind of relationship, if any, existed between Leonard and his stepbrother Dwight, but it is interesting to note the parallels in their lives, as both graduated from high school and attended further schooling, and both were in the Army Air Corps during World War II, with Dwight becoming a bombardier and Leonard a navigator. Unlike Leonard, Dwight survived the war, exiting with the rank of major and eventually settling in Rock Springs, Wyoming.[63]

According to his school and military records, Leonard used the Fisher last name during his youth, although there is no evidence that his stepfather adopted him or that his legal last name was changed from Phillips to Fisher.[64] The family moved frequently, and Leonard attended schools in Orleans, Nebraska; Norton, Kansas; Goodland, Kansas; and Clayton, Kansas.[65]

Leonard Harvey Phillips's 1938 senior high school portrait. *Courtesy of Ann Gallentine.*

Leonard graduated from Clayton Rural High School in 1938 with eight other students.[66] His classmates remembered him being tall (military records show he was six feet, three inches tall), quiet and intelligent. He had no time for girlfriends or parties; rather, he was determined to be successful in business.[67] For a short time, he attended Grand Island Business College in Grand Island, Nebraska, but did not make it to graduation.[68] He then worked for Montgomery Ward and the Chicago, Rock Island and Pacific Railroad doing general labor duties while earning between seventy and eighty-four dollars per month.[69] His classmates thought his stepfather, Dwight, was his supervisor at the railroad.[70]

Leonard enlisted in the army in January 1940, and it seems it was at this time that he started to use his legal last name, Phillips.[71] He was described as being tall and lean, with blue eyes, blond hair and a light complexion. He completed a personal history statement at the time of his enlistment, and his written responses were very succinct. He noted no scars or distinguishing marks, no stepparents (perhaps his relationship with Dwight had not been a happy one), no siblings, no memberships or participation in social societies and no honors, hobbies or pastimes. He also listed incorrect information about his biological father (the wrong birth year and whether he was alive or deceased), and a guess could be made that he did not know his paternal information well. He noted that he spoke no languages besides English, had never traveled outside the United States, had no experience as an entertainer or instructor and had no special skills in photography, public speaking or cryptanalysis, and he listed his athletic skills as being "average."[72]

Appointed as a private first class in June 1940, Leonard was moved up to the rank of sergeant by that December. He worked as a clerk at Letterman

Clayton Rural High School's 1938 senior class of ten. *Courtesy Ann Gallentine.*

Army Hospital in San Francisco, California.[73] Because of his extended military service (compared to his other crewmates), more records are available for Phillips.

He may have been a little accident-prone, as he managed to get into poison oak while hiking near Sea Cliff in San Francisco and was told to put some calamine lotion on the itchy rash.[74] He later also fell off some steps drastically enough to knock himself out cold with a concussion, which gained him a short stay in the hospital.[75] And in a different event, he had to get stitches on his left thumb while on duty.[76]

Leonard requested to transfer to the Army Air Corps in early 1942 and began the process of attending multiple schools and training programs. We know this transfer occurred because Leonard applied for appointment as an aviation cadet on March 9, 1942. Even though he was twenty years old and already had almost two years of military service, his mother had to approve his application and sign it as his guardian.[77] Leonard also needed character references to make this transition, and he received at least three from his superiors at Letterman General Hospital. Captain Frank R. Day and Majors John D. Foley and Richard E. Humes all wrote that they had known Leonard for various lengths of time and that he was of excellent character and habits and well-qualified to be a flying cadet.[78]

By April 20, his application had been approved, as he was found to be mentally, morally and physically qualified.[79] In July, he was with the Provisional Aviation Cadet Company at Mather Field, California, where he was appointed to an aviation cadet and transferred to Kelly Field, Texas.[80] While stationed at Hondo, Texas, he was appointed for training to be a second lieutenant, and his military serial number changed to reflect this advancement to an officer's rank.[81] While there, he completed courses in Ground School Dead Reckoning, Ground School Celestial, Total Navigational Ground School and Total Meteorology.

By early October 1942, Leonard had received certification that he could be trained in the operation and maintenance of secret and confidential equipment.[82]

The navigator's position was one of substantial importance and heavy responsibility for obvious reasons. According to the *B-17 Pilot Training Manual*, navigation is defined as "determining geographic positions by means of (a) pilotage, (b) dead reckoning, (c) radio, or (d) celestial navigation, or any combination of these 4 methods. By any one or combination of methods the navigator determines the position of the airplane in relation to the earth." Pilotage is using the ground to navigate, which means the navigator had to be able to see the terrain below and identify landmarks or geographical features. Dead reckoning is done by tracking distance and time flown and verifying these things with navigational readings and visual checks. Radio navigation is exactly what it sounds like: using the onboard radio to check in at various points. Celestial navigation is done by referencing two or more celestial bodies during nighttime.[83] In simple words, the navigator needed to know exactly where his plane was at all times.

On April 15, 1943, Leonard was rated as an aircraft observer, aerial navigator, after a board review of his and his fellow cadets' training performances.[84] Leonard's actual flight time was not lengthy at this point in his training, however, as in March, he had only completed eleven training flights (which was noted in a physical exam for flying because he suffered from airsickness during four of those flights).[85] On April 23, 1943, he was given orders to go to Ephrata, Washington, with the 395th Bomb Group, a day after he had been commissioned to the rank of second lieutenant.[86] He received good grades in his courses at Hondo and graduated on April 22, 1943, ranking 50th in a class of 216.[87]

On May 28, 1943, Leonard completed a designation of beneficiary document while at Walla Walla Army Air Base, in which he named his grandmother Frances Caldwell of Norton, Kansas, to be his main beneficiary, with his mother, now known as Libby Brown of Dupont, Colorado, as secondary.[88]

Leonard is a prime example of how quickly the U.S. military was turning out new crews—he had received his promotion to second lieutenant only two months prior to the crash. When his remains were recovered (only his torso could be found) from the crash site in 1945, there were U.S. Marine Corps sergeant chevrons, nine snapshots, a package of school report cards and miscellaneous papers in his pockets.[89] Perhaps he had exchanged military mementos with a marine corps buddy to acquire the chevrons, a common form of acknowledging friendship or keeping mementos of a time or experience.

5

CHARLES HULBERT SUPPES III

Second Lieutenant, Bombardier, 0733366

Called "Suppie" by those who knew him, Charles Suppes III was the only son of Charles II and Natalie (Crissman) Suppes. His sister, Natalie, was nine years older than he. Born on April 25, 1920, and raised in Johnstown, Pennsylvania, Suppie enjoyed drawing cartoons and wanted to join the military.[90] His father was in the coal industry, and his mother was a nurse, according to their 1910 marriage certificate. Charles H. Suppes II passed away suddenly of a cerebral hemorrhage when Suppie was only ten. A few years later, his mother, Natalie, married Carl Geis, a World War I veteran who also lived in Johnstown.[91]

Suppie was an active student at Westmont–Upper Yoder High School, writing for the school paper called *The Yodler*, working as an editor on the *Phoenician* yearbook and participating in the mixed chorus singing group, drama club and Hi-Y club, which was an organization affiliated with the Young Men's Christian Association, or YMCA, for middle and high school students with a mission to "create, maintain and extend, throughout the home, school, and community, high standards of Christian character."[92] His classmates described him as "bubbling with nonsense—court jester" in his senior yearbook.

Charles Hulbert Suppes III with his bombardier's wings badge, officer's lapel pins and ribbons for two of his medals. *Suppes family collection.*

He won honors for a humorous article he wrote while on the newspaper staff in 1936–37.[93]

Suppes entered the armed forces and underwent various trainings at multiple locations. As noted in the dedication program for a memorial chapel named in his honor in Johnstown after his death, he was a good student.[94]

> *On May 10, 1939, he received an appointment to the Air Force Technical School at Chanute Field, Rantoul, Illinois, and enlisted in the Army Air Force. He graduated there February 9, 1940, and was stationed at Mitchell Field as radio operator on a bomber. He passed a competitive examination at Mitchell Field which enabled him to study celestial navigation and meteorology and on February 1, 1941, he was made a Sergeant and sent to Cochran Field, Georgia. He was an instructor there until he won another competitive examination for cadet training and was sent on March 29, 1942, to Santa Ana, California as a Flying Cadet. Upon completing his course there he was selected to be sent to the Advanced Flying School at Kirtland Field, New Mexico. On November 21, 1942, he was graduated as a master bombardier and second lieutenant, being sixth highest in a class of 500. He was stationed on Pacific Defense Patrol until the crew of his Flying Fortress, the* Scharazad, *were given orders to join a squadron which was leaving for England.*

There are descendants of Suppie's relatives still living in the Johnstown area, and even though he has been gone for many years, a number of his cartoons and possessions have been passed down and are cherished by the family.[95]

As the bombardier, Suppie would have been responsible for conducting the bombing once they were in Europe. This meant that he needed to have a thorough understanding of speed, altitude, direction, drift, bomb speed and any possible variations in order to hit the determined target(s) with accuracy. The bombardier was also expected to know the duties of the navigator and have the ability to step into that position should the navigator become incapacitated.[96] This explains why Suppes underwent such intensive training.

After Suppie's death, his mother commissioned an oil portrait by Loris Withers in 1945. The painting contains interesting information, as it shows Suppes wearing a selection of medals (two are also shown in his formal military portrait as well) that is of interest. He had the bombardier badge metal "wings" pin, which was issued between 1918 and 1949, presented

The Wyoming Bomber Crash of 1943

Suppie drew this for a friend who had experienced an appendectomy. (Note the appendix in a jar being observed by friends!) *Suppes family collection.*

upon completion of basic flight training and bomber instruction.[97] He also received the Army Good Conduct, American Defense Service and American Campaign Medals. The Army Good Conduct Medal was awarded to those who served during three years of peacetime or one year of wartime. Air force personnel were issued the army's version of this medal until 1963.[98] The American Defense Service Medal was awarded to people who served between September 8, 1939, and December 7, 1941, for at least a year.[99] The American Campaign Medal was awarded to those who served domestically between December 7, 1941, and March 2, 1946.[100]

Sadly, it took almost eight years for the World War II Veterans Compensation Bureau to approve the compensation for Suppie's death. Full compensation was $500, which was to be sent to his parents.[101]

6

JAMES ALFRED HINDS

Technical Sergeant, Aircraft Engineer/Top Turret Gunner, 39246908

James Alfred Hinds was born on June 14, 1918, to Vesta (Richardson) Hinds and Moses Hinds in Grove, Oklahoma, and grew into a slim five-foot-eight-inch-tall man with a ruddy complexion, gray eyes and brown hair.[102] He and his sister, Ruth, and brothers, India and Edwin, were raised in El Reno, Oklahoma, and he graduated from El Reno High School in 1938.[103] He went by his middle name, Alfred. Vesta and Moses divorced during Alfred's youth, and Vesta remarried sometime after. Alfred was active in sports, wrestling and playing football for the school. A copy of the *El Reno Daily Tribune* from October 1936 shows a photograph of the "Cridermen," that is, the football players of Coach Frank Crider's team, as they prepared to take on their opposition: the Classen Comets. Hinds is visible in the front row, but his number is obscured.[104]

There were forty-four young men from El Reno High School who served during World War II. In 2019, the Memorial Stadium at the school was rededicated to the forty-four servicemen as the culmination of a history project conducted by teacher Brian Rukes and his students, who had researched the biographies of the men. Although many decades have passed since Alfred and his family resided in El Reno, it is impressive that the community has diligently honored the memory of James Alfred Hinds.[105]

Descendants feel the family may have moved west for work and believe a female relative worked at the Douglas Aircraft plant in Long Beach, California.[106] Alfred was drafted while living in Hermosa Beach, California, an area in which he spent the last few years of his life with his family. The

1940 census shows him living in Hermosa Beach with his mother and two of his siblings and notes that he was working as an aircraft mechanic apprentice. By June 1943, he was married to Georgia Pauline Williams, who went by Pauline, and she was newly pregnant when Alfred died with their only child, John James, who was born in February 1944.[107] Family memories indicate that Alfred knew of the pregnancy, and one cannot help but wonder if he and copilot Tony Tilotta discussed fatherhood during the short time they knew each other.[108]

James Alfred Hinds's 1938 El Reno High School senior portrait. *Courtesy of El Reno High School.*

Alfred's family may have left El Reno, Oklahoma, but they were not forgotten. The September 17, 1944 edition of the *El Reno Daily Tribune*, ran this article:

Sergeant Hinds Declared Dead

Technical Sergeant James Alfred Hinds, graduate of El Reno high school in the class of 1938, has been officially declared dead by the war department, friends here have learned.

Sergeant Hinds entered the army air forces in June 1942 and was serving as engineer on a Flying Fortress that disappeared June 28, 1943, while en route from Pendleton, Ore., to Grand Island, Neb. No trace was ever found of the plane or its crew.

Listed missing for a year, Sergeant Hinds was declared dead by the war department on June 30.

He was the son of Mrs. Vesta Wolfenbarger of Redondo Beach, Calif., formerly of El Reno. His wife and baby son, John James, reside in Hermosa Beach, Calif. Two brothers, Marvin and Eddie, are serving in the army.

Sergeant Hinds lived in El Reno with his parents for many years, moving to California shortly after his graduation from high school here.

According to a letter from Vesta, her children's father died when they were very young, and she was very close to her sons.[109] She may have been referring to their stepfather, John Robert Wolfenbarger, who passed away in 1928, when Alfred was about ten years old.

In 1945, when the crash site and bodies were found, the *Manhattan Beach News* reported the discovery and noted that Alfred left behind two brothers, India and Edwin; a sister, Ruth Stout; and his mother, Vesta Wolfenbarger (sometimes mistakenly recorded as Wolfenburger).[110] An easy guess is that Edwin and Eddie were the same person and that India, Marvin and Marilin were one and the same, as Vesta referenced having two sons besides Alfred.

The *Manhattan Beach News* printed on August 28, 1945, a story about the wreckage recovery and made the (rather outrageous) claim that the plane was the "last of the unaccounted-for planes which had been lost in the United States."[111] The same article claimed Alfred had lived most of his life in California, which is not accurate, but the significance of honoring a local life lost is admirable and was surely appreciated by his loved ones.

As the aircraft engineer, Alfred was responsible for knowing the aircraft inside and out. He would have tracked the fuel consumption, verified the bombs were loaded correctly, cleaned and serviced the machine guns and potentially assisted with operating radio equipment. The engineer was also responsible for manning the top gun turret during battle.[112]

Pauline remarried in the spring of 1950 in Yuma, Arizona.[113] With her new husband, Howard Gray, she raised John James, who also eventually became a flight engineer in the U.S. Air Force.

As World War II ended, many veterans' organizations across the United States began the sad task of compiling information about their regional residents who had been lost or killed in the war. The American Legion Post 184 of Redondo Beach was one such place where they compiled information about and photographs of those who had served, including James Alfred Hinds. Over the years, a lot of the information fell by the wayside, but recent efforts by members of the post, in conjunction with the Manhattan Beach Historical Society, have resulted in a renewed recognition and appreciation for the area's veterans.[114]

7

FERGUSON THEODORE BELL III

Technical Sergeant, Radio Operator/Radio Hatch Gunner, 34334803

Ferguson Bell was technically the third of his name, but he appears to have used the "Jr." suffix, as his grandfather had died long before he was born.[115] Called "Ferg" by family and friends (and in this publication), he was born on November 25, 1921, to Ferguson Theodore Sr. (II) (hereafter called Ferguson) and Frances (Dunning) Bell in Thomasville, Alabama.[116] Ferg's father's side of the family was Irish, and his paternal grandparents had immigrated to the United States in 1894. It is charming to note that his paternal grandmother was named Theodora Sweeney but apparently used the nickname Dora. Once she married Ferg's grandfather, she became Dora Bell, and that may be the most "adora-bell" fluke.[117]

Ferg's father, Ferguson, was from Philadelphia, Pennsylvania, and attended the Williamson Free School of Mechanical Trades. His 1917 school yearbook identified him as a bricklayer.[118] He served in the U.S. Naval Reserve during World War I, spending about half a year in France while on active duty. He was honorably discharged in April 1922.

Ferg's mother, Frances, hailed from Alabama but was in Wyoming working for a telephone company and living with her brother Thomas and his family in Shoshoni, Wyoming, by 1920. The census from that year also lists a Frances Dunning of Alabama who worked as a telephone operator while living in a boardinghouse in Riverton, Wyoming, so Frances may have been counted in that census twice (or there was another person with a lot of similarities just twenty-two miles away).[119] Frances Dunning married

Ferguson T. Bell Sr. in 1920 in Riverton, Wyoming. Their marriage certificate notes they both resided in Riverton and shows the marriage was witnessed by Alice Reece and Mrs. C.B. Boddy, but it does not provide any family information.[120] Ferg's mother seems to have been a woman who was efficient and self-reliant.

However Ferguson and Frances met while in Wyoming, they made their married life together by moving around the nation in the following years. In 1925, the family was in Charleston, South Carolina, where Ferguson was working as a superintendent of a construction company.[121] In 1930, they were in Monticello Village, New York, where Ferguson was working as a building contractor.[122] By 1935, they were in Newark, New Jersey.[123] In 1937, Frances and Ferguson divorced in Florida and went their separate ways, with Ferguson returning to New Jersey while Frances and Ferg went back to Alabama.[124]

Ferguson Theodore Bell Jr. Courtesy Patsy Sessions via Find a Grave.

Ferg attended high school in Thomasville, Alabama, where he was a "star player on the high school football team," according to an article from *The Selma Times-Journal* of August 19, 1945. He graduated in 1939 and attended a junior college in New Jersey for a short time.[125] The 1940 census records then show that Ferg was living with his mother, Frances, and grandparents Lee and Rebecca Dunning in Thomasville that year and that he was working as a deliveryman in the beer industry at the age of eighteen.[126]

When Lee Dunning passed away in January 1945, the Dunning family had already lost two of their own to the war: Ferg, still missing at the point, and one of Ferg's cousins, Clyde Austin Dunning, who died in June 1942 while serving in the merchant marine when his ship, the SS *Sam Houston*, was attacked by a German U-boat between Antigua and the British Virgin Islands.[127]

Ferg's military records describe him as being five feet, eight inches tall and weighing 182 pounds, with blue eyes and brown hair.[128] He was drafted in July 1942, and by February 1943, he was still at the rank of private while stationed at Tyndall Field, Florida.[129]

As the radio operator, Ferg was responsible for all communications. The same as it was at any time in history, communication was a vital aspect of World War II warfare. The radio operator also needed to know how to perform any needed maintenance and small repairs to the radio equipment. Along with this, he was to operate the machine gun near his position.[130]

When the wreckage was found, *The Sheridan Press* reported on August 15, 1945, that Ferg's parents were from Baraboo, Wisconsin:

> *Mr. and Mrs. Ferguson T. Bell of Baraboo, WI waited today in Casper for information on the wreckage of a plane found in the Big Horn mountains of Northern Wyoming. They seek some trace of Ferguson T. Bell, Jr. 20, a radio operator on a B-17 that disappeared two years ago on a flight from Pendleton, Ore., to Grand Island, Neb.*

It is likely that the newspaper staff did not know that the "Mrs. Bell" referred to here was Ferg's stepmother, Kathryn.[131]

The *Casper Star-Tribune* offered more to the story of Ferg's parents being in Wyoming looking for him when it reported on August 15, 1945 (VJ Day,[132] or Victory over Japan Day, which officially marked the end of World War II after President Harry Truman announced the Japanese surrender):

> *Seek Clue to Plane Missing Two Years*
> *Son May Have Lost Life in Big Horn Air Crash*
>
> *Mr. and Mrs. Ferguson T. Bell of Baraboo, Wis., waited in Casper today for information on the wreckage of a plane found in the Big Horn mountains of northern Wyoming.*
>
> *They seek some trace of Ferguson T. Bell Jr., 20, radio operator on a B-17 that disappeared two years ago on a flight from Pendleton, Ore., to Grand Island, Neb.*
>
> *They visited Rapid City, S.D., Billings, Mont., and Sheridan Wyo., without success. They stopped at the closed Casper Army Air Field and told their story to a guard. He informed them of an Associated Press story in Monday's* Tribune-Herald *that wreckage of a plane which apparently crashed a year or so ago had been found near Cloud peak.*
>
> *Mr. Bell said he believed it might be the plane on which their son was riding and they will stay here until information is released on the wreckage in northern Wyoming.*

The Wyoming Bomber Crash of 1943

The next article in the same column reads, in part:

Plane Identified as Army Craft

Sheridan, Wyo., Aug. 15, AP—Wreckage discovered high in the Big Horn mountains of northern Wyoming has been identified as that of an army plane, headquarters of Big Horn National forest disclosed today. The forest service office here said decomposed bodies found near the plane were being brought down the East slope of the mountains to Buffalo and would be taken by ambulance to the Rapid City, S.D., Army Air base.

An expanded article from the *Casper Star-Tribune* a few days later, August 19, 1945, provided more information about the Bells' time in Wyoming, noting that they had traveled through Rapid City, South Dakota, through northeastern Wyoming and southern Montana to eventually land in Casper, where they were when the discovery was made official. They turned around and returned to Rapid City, as that was where the remains were being sent. The horrific task of identifying Ferg landed on Ferguson while they were there. The article noted that although the outcome was unfortunate, the family could at least know where their son had died, and:

While in Casper Mr. Bell recounted that even before they knew that a plane had been discovered on Cloud Peak that mountain had some sort of attraction for them. Whenever they drove within sighting distance of it their eyes were drawn to the peak, sometimes in clouds and other times shining in the sun. They believed it was a premonition.

Ferg's remains were scheduled to arrive in Thomasville, Alabama, by August 21, 1945, and on August 22, his family held a funeral service for him.[133]

Last Rites Held for Thomasville Flyer

Thomasville, Ala., Aug. 23, 1945—Funeral services for S-Sgt. Ferguson T. Bell, a casualty of a plane crash on Cloud Peak, Wyoming, June 29, 1943, were held at the Thomasville Baptist Church, Wednesday afternoon. Dr. John G. Hutchinson, pastor of the church, was [officiant]. He was assisted by the Rev. Chas. A. Corbitt and Chaplain N.V. Sack, of Craig Field. Members of the Thomasville Post, American Legion, attended in a body. A military escort, accompanied by a firing squad from Craig Field took part in the graveside rites. Internment was made at Choctaw Corner cemetery.

The remains of Sgt. Bell among the ten bodies found among the plane wreckage August 10th were identified by his father, F.T. Bell of Newark, N.J. Radioman on this plane Sgt. Bell had flashed a message that the plane had encountered bad weather when near Capar [Casper], Wyoming, after taking off from an Oregon field. All searches of the army air force had failed to find any trace of the missing plane. After a year Sgt. Bell's mother, Mrs. Frances Dunning Bell, of Little Rock, was notified by the war department that her son was considered dead. Another year passed before the plane wreck was discovered on a snow-capped mountain of Wyoming.

Sgt. Bell was 21 at the time of his death. It was at his request that his remains were sent here, his boyhood home, for burial. Among the survivors in addition to his parents, is his grandmother.

By 1946, Frances was working in Little Rock, Arkansas. It was during this time she applied for a grave marker for Ferg, and she noted in the application that she would like the marker sent to her brother Will Dunning in Thomasville, Alabama, as he would be available to receive it.[134]

8

LEE VAUGHAN MILLER

Sergeant, Assistant Aircraft Engineer/Waist Gunner, 35433022

Lee Vaughan Miller was born on October 21, 1918, to Wilson Roscoe and Nancy Minerva (Wolfe) Miller. He grew up to be a slender young man with brown eyes, black hair and a fair complexion, standing at five feet, eight inches tall. (Or he grew up to be a slender young man with blue eyes, light brown hair and a fair complexion, standing five feet, ten inches tall—his service records contain varying descriptions.) Family memories are that he had blue eyes and light brown hair and that he was closer to six feet tall, which seems most likely when viewing photographs of him and his brothers.[135] There is also lingering confusion about his name—some of his military records list "Vaughan Lee Miller," but his headstone (approved by the family) reads "Lee Vaughan Miller." Postcards he sent to his family indicate his legal name was Lee Vaughan Miller but that he went by Vaughan.[136] The Millers were a close-knit family with five children: Annie, Sherman, Howard, Clarence and Vaughan, the youngest.[137] Vaughan's father worked many years as a payroll clerk for the area coal mines and encouraged his sons to do anything other than coal mining, as he had seen the health issues caused by the industry in miners.[138]

After graduating with twenty-six others from Trap Hill High School in Surveyor, West Virginia, in May 1937, Vaughan spent two years working for the Civilian Conservation Corps (CCC), enrolling just days before his twenty-first birthday.[139] Records from this time note that Vaughan was a field leader who performed "very satisfactory" work, with only one noted reprimand.

The Wyoming Bomber Crash of 1943

Lee Vaughan Miller holding a machine gun. *Courtesy of the Jim Gatchell Memorial Museum.*

This admonishment came after Vaughan left camp without permission with some of "the boys" to check out the area's radio station. His absence without leave resulted in him losing a day's pay. Family memories help fill in the story of what may have occurred on this day. Some of Vaughan's brothers were members of a small local band called the Malden Valley Boys, and it seems

43

likely that Vaughan took the trip to listen to them while they performed in a guest appearance on the Beckley, West Virginia radio station WJLS. Interestingly, one of their Trap Hill High School classmates, James Cecil Dickens, was a frequent feature on that station. He would go on to be better known as Little Jimmy Dickens, a famous country music singer and member of the *Grand Ole Opry*.[140]

Although Vaughan's CCC records are minimal at best, they do contain a rather interesting side story. On October 12, 1940, there was an incident outside of the CCC camp in which Vaughan was injured. On the evening of October 12, Vaughan visited the Top Hat Roadhouse, where he was attacked by several civilians who used beer bottles to knock him unconscious. They then kicked Vaughan on his torso and literally jumped on his left arm. Vaughan suffered numerous lacerations on his head and face and contusions on his chest and left arm. Witnesses Claude Johnson and Carl Miser verified Vaughan's account of the event, noting that the instigator was a man named Newman and verifying that no conversation between Vaughan and Newman had occurred prior to the attack. On the night in question, Vaughan was on "pass for the evening," meaning he had permission to be out of the camp. One G.G. Newman of Beaver, West Virginia, was held by the civil authorities while he awaited trial for the assault. Vaughan was officially absolved of any blame regarding the incident in January the following year.

Vaughan had a substantial amount of his pay from his time in the CCC sent home, and in his enrollment records, it was noted that his mother, Minerva, needed medical care, which required additional financial income beyond what the family farm was generating. Prior to his time with the CCC, Vaughan had worked as a truck driver. During his time with the CCC, he participated in a variety of activities and classes, including etiquette, music, forestry, conservation, health and safety, photography, leadership and typing.[141]

Like his other crew members, Vaughan was sent to numerous training camps around the country after his induction into the military. He was drafted on June 13, 1942, and by that July, he was stationed at Keesler Field, Mississippi.[142] The next month, he was at Curtiss-Wright Technical Institute in Glendale, California.[143] A local newspaper reported that by December 1942, he had completed a course on the West Coast in "airplane construction," which was likely his training at the Curtiss-Wright Technical Institute.[144] Vaughan also would have gone through gunnery training, and he may have done this at Wendover Aerial Gunnery School in Utah.[145]

As the assistant aircraft engineer, Vaughan would have been the backup for James Alfred Hinds and would have needed to know and understand the aircraft just as thoroughly. He also would have manned one of the waist gunner positions during battle.[146]

Vaughan returned home to visit family during his last leave, spending much of that time with his fiancée, Ruth Hanocker. They had planned to get married during that time but were prevented from doing so because a bridge in their area had been washed out and Vaughan did not have enough leave time to accommodate the additional travel.[147]

Like so many families during the war, the Miller family sent more than one son into the armed forces, with Vaughan's brother Clarence also a part of the military at the time of Vaughan's death. The *Raleigh Register* of Beckley, West Virginia, reported:

Glen Daniel Flier Declared Dead After Missing a Year

Staff Sgt. Lee Vaughan Miller has been declared officially dead, as of June 30, 1944, according to a message from the war department to his parents, Mr. and Mrs. W.R. Miller, of Glen Daniel.

Previously they were notified that he was missing after the plane on which he was serving apparently disappeared while in flight over central Wyoming. This message was received August 1, 1943.

The parents said they learned from the war department that a message was received from the ship at midnight of June 28, 1943. Nothing further was disclosed, leaving the parents to presume that neither plane nor crew members were found.

The 25-year-old staff sergeant was graduated from Trap Hill high school in 1937. He worked for two and a half years with the Civilian Conservation corps before induction into the army air force June 13, 1942.

He received his basic training at Keesler Field, Miss., and was graduated from the Curtiss Wright Technical school November 25, 1942.

He was transferred to Washington, then was sent to Pendleton Field, Oregon. He was en route from Pendleton Field to Grand Island, Nebraska, when the plane disappeared.

He is survived by one sister, Mrs. Annie Maynor, of Harper, and three brothers, Cpl. Clarence Miller, of Michigan, Sherman Miller, of Glen Daniel, and Howard Miller, of Liberty, Ky.

Vaughan and his fiancée, Ruth, circa spring 1943. *Miller family collection.*

By the summer of 1945, the Miller family had dealt with Vaughan's absence for two years, but according to neighbors, they had not quite given up the hope that he could still be alive.[148] When the wreckage was found in August, their hopes were dashed.

The *Raleigh Register* of Beckley, West Virginia, reported on August 24, 1945:

MILLER, Staff Sergeant Lee Vaughan: age 25 years, of Glen Daniel, son of Mr. and Mrs. Wilson R. Miller was identified among army airmen found entombed in their flying fortress which crashed in Big Horn Mountain in the Wyoming Rockies, June 28, 1943. The body will arrive at Prince, Wednesday, August 22nd at 6:49 p.m. and will be escorted by Staff Sergeant Gordon B. Porterfield. It will be then removed to the Calfee Funeral Home where it will remain until 10:30 a.m. Thursday, then to be removed to the residence. Funeral services will be conducted Friday, August 24th at the Mt. Tabor Baptist Church at 2:30 p.m. with Rev. B.C. Jennings officiating. Burial will follow in the Calfee cemetery. Arrangements by Calfee Funeral Home.

9

CHARLES EDGAR NEWBURN JR.

Sergeant, Assistant Radio Operator/Ball Turret Gunner, 38188183

Junior or Charley, as he was known, was born in Wister, Oklahoma, to Charles Edgar Newburn Sr. and Helen (Myers) Newburn on December 14, 1921.[149] His birth was quite likely extra special, as Helen's birthday was December 13.[150] Junior was the oldest of three brothers. According to family memory, Junior played piano and guitar and grew up to work in his uncle's general store as a clerk. When he was sixteen, he made a cedar chest for his mother. He graduated from Wister High School and was engaged to be married to Frances Swafford, a young woman whom the family remembered as being lovely.

When Newburn left for training, his friends and family held a going away party, where his grandparents and other family members were present. That same day, Junior gave his mother some pink depression glass items he had purchased for her as a gift.[151]

Like those in the other assistant positions (copilot, assistant aircraft engineer and assistant gunner), the assistant radio operator needed to have the ability to step into the main position should that man become incapacitated. Junior also would have been

Charles Edgar Newburn. *Newburn family collection.*

Junior with his mother, Helen, during his last visit home. *Newburn family collection.*

the person manning the ball turret, a position beneath the radio room. Gunners were expected to be precise in their aircraft identification skills and have solid marksmanship abilities, and they needed to be confident and knowledgeable about the machine guns.[152] According to the *Duties and Responsibilities, B-17 Pilot Training Manual 1943*, "power turret gunners require many mental and physical qualities similar to what we know as inherent flying ability, since the operation of the power turret and gunsight are much like that of airplane flight operation."

By late February 1943, Junior had been promoted to staff sergeant. The *Poteau News* reported:

Charles Newburn, Jr. Promoted to Sergeant

The graduation and promotion to staff sergeant of Charles Newburn, Jr., son of Mr. and Mrs. Charley Newburn of Wister, has been announced at the AAF flexible gunnery school, Fort Myers, Fla., by Col. Delmar T. Spivey, commanding officer of the school.

Staff sergeant Newburn has just completed an intensive five week's course of instruction in the operation of the large guns that arm American planes against tanks.

Junior had undergone training at Sioux Falls, South Dakota; Fort Myers, Florida; and Blythe, California.[153] The Sioux Falls Army Technical School was created in the spring of 1942, with trainees beginning work before the base was complete. Radio operators received instruction in communications, including Morse code and radio maintenance. More than half of the radio operators who served on B-17 and B-24 aircraft during the war trained at this site.[154] Fort Myers Army Airfield was located in Charlotte County, Florida, and included the Fort Myers Bombing and Gunnery Range, where soldiers trained on a variety of bombing and gunnery techniques.[155] Blythe Army Airfield was a part of the Desert Training Center in the Sonoran Desert, and by 1943, it was a base for training heavy bombardment crews.[156]

After the recovery of the crew members' bodies in 1945, the remains were sent to their families for closure and burial. The Newburn family remembered a military escort bringing Junior's body back on a train. The casket with Junior's remains was taken to his grandmother's house and placed in the living room for visitation before his burial at Maxey Cemetery in his hometown of Wister, Oklahoma.[157] He was survived by his parents, grandmothers and brothers.

10

JAKE FLOYD PENICK

Sergeant, Aircraft Gunner, 18008587

Jake Floyd Penick was born on May 14, 1921, in Waneta, Texas, to John William Penick Jr. and Lena Pearl (Scoggin) Penick. One of at least seven children, Jake had five brothers and two sisters and worked on the family farm during his youth.[158] It is likely that the Penick family felt the effects of the Great Depression in a visceral manner, as opportunities for employment were slim. The area of Houston County where the Penick family lived was agriculture-based, with many small towns established to serve the needs of farm families.[159]

Jake attended the Waneta School in his early years and graduated from Grapeland High School in nearby Grapeland, Texas, in 1938.[160] The 1940 census shows that his older brother Jack was working as a truck driver for a pepper mill while still living at home with their parents, siblings and an uncle. Jake was noted as being in the Civilian Conservation Corps (CCC), working in reforestation, while also being counted as a part of the Penick family home.[161]

In April 1940, Jake enlisted in the CCC and had twenty-two dollars of his monthly pay sent to his father. His reason for wanting to join the CCC was to "further education and aid family." Jake's CCC records contain several mistakes that appear to have originated from the person who completed the form, so it is difficult to ascertain exact information about his home situation, amount of high school completed and previous work experience. One reason it is likely the blame lies at the hands of the typist includes this mistake: according to CCC documents, Penick's previous work experience began in

May 1940 and ended in September 1939—surely that was a clerical error. CCC records also contain conflicting entries regarding the type of previous work experience Penick had, with one page showing he had "always" worked for his father on the family farm, while another shows he had experience as a "loader" working for a Mr. Glynn Haberly, and yet another record shows he had worked for the Habony Box Factory in 1937. The dates during which he attended high school also vary within the records, and his mother's name is misspelled.[162]

Jake's physical description, however, is consistent across the records: he was five feet, eleven inches tall, weighed 182 pounds and had brown hair, brown eyes and a ruddy complexion. He performed road construction work during his time with the CCC and was stationed at a camp at Ratcliff, Texas.[163] The camp was located in eastern Texas, a region that had experienced such heavy timber cutting that the area was considered deforested. Members of the CCC camp planted trees and built roads in the newly named Davy Crockett National Forest. They also constructed recreational areas, installed telephone lines, built one fire lookout tower and dismantled another and repaired a dam, among other activities.[164] It is interesting to note that Jake was listed as having gone AWOP (absent without pay) from July 8 to July 22, 1940, and AWOL (absent without leave) from July 23 to July 29, 1940, which coincided with the last day of his service in the CCC. In spite of this, Jake received good remarks in his records, which included rating the men on their personality qualifications, physical health, attitude in camp, avocational interests and more. Along with these "good" remarks, it was noted that Jake was interested in football.[165]

It seems most of his brothers, if not all, also served in the military. When Jake left the CCC in July 1940, he enlisted in the military, which seems to be the reason for his absence from the CCC camp, as he was probably traveling to the enlistment office to complete paperwork.[166] Eventually, he was stationed at Fort Sill, Oklahoma, for training at the same time his older brother Jack was stationed there. Family stories say that Jack met a young woman named Iva Lorene Floyd, and they became an item.[167] Iva had been widowed when she was very young and was working as a waitress in a café

Jake Floyd Penick. Penick family collection.

while raising her daughter, Jolene.[168] Eventually, Iva introduced her beau's brother Jake to her friend Dorothy Jo Gray, and sparks must have flown, as those two soon became sweethearts. There was a double wedding event on August 2, 1941, with both couples being each other's witnesses.[169]

Jake's position of aircraft gunner meant that, in addition to operating a waist gun, he was responsible for maintenance and repairs to armament, gunsights, bomb racks and more.[170]

Although Jake and Dorothy Jo were married for almost two years, some of Jake's military records were not updated to reflect that fact by the time of his death in June 1943. This may have added an extra layer of frustration for his family upon the disappearance of the aircraft. After the discovery of the remains in 1945, Jake's body and any identified effects were sent to his parents in Texas, where he wished to be buried.[171]

11

LEWIS MARVIN SHEPARD

Staff Sergeant, Assistant Aircraft Gunner, 14083794

Tall, dark and handsome. That might be how the young women from the Jacksonville, Florida roller rink would have remembered the six-foot-one-inch-tall, lean young man with black hair and green eyes who was outgoing and friendly.[172] Born on May 26, 1921, in Greensboro, Florida, Lewis was David and Leo Hazel (Crosby) Shepard's second child, following his brother David (Vernon). Siblings Elsie Mae, Jack, James Arlington and Thomas Alva all followed between then and 1930.[173] As Lewis grew up, he wanted to be a printer. After high school, he apprenticed for a local printer and then joined the merchant marine.[174] On October 4, 1942, he enlisted in the army air corps.[175]

Prior to leaving for military training, Lewis enjoyed hunting, fishing and roller skating. He apparently found the roller rink to be a useful place to meet young women and kept a little brown book full of women's names, telephone numbers, physical descriptions and personal comments. Some of his comments were "an old sweetheart now a good friend," "red head," "nice looking," "the gal with the golden hair," "nice and then some" and "O'Boy."

Lewis's brothers also served in the military. Thomas Alva was stationed in Okinawa, Japan, while David Vernon was a marine who served in Guam, U.S. Territorial Island, and later became a stunt pilot. James Arlington was a firefighter in the naval reserve, and Jack served in the air force and wanted to be a pilot, but the war ended before he saw any service.[176] The Shepard boys took care of their mother and sister after their father left the family while dealing with his own struggles.[177]

Lewis underwent training at a variety of military bases, including Camp Blanding, Florida; Lowry Field, Colorado; Harlingen Aerial Gunnery School in Harlingen, Texas; Air Corps Technical School at Keesler Field, Mississippi; and the Army Air Base at Ephrata, Washington. He graduated from the U.S. Air Forces Technical School's aircraft armorers' course at Lowry Field on January 16, 1943, and sent his diploma home to his mother for safe keeping.[178] During this course, Lewis learned how to perform maintenance operations and repairs on the airplane armament, which included machine guns, gun turrets, the bombsight and the automatic pilot. The following month, he became an aerial gunner and achieved the rank of staff sergeant while at Harlingen Aerial Gunnery School in Texas. Lewis was not in any one place for long.[179]

Lewis Marvin Shepard. *Shepard family collection.*

The assistant gunner position was like the aircraft gunner in duties but also included manning the tail gun position. It is difficult to imagine the six-foot-one-inch-tall Lewis folded into the cramped tail gun space.[180] The *Official AAF Guide* notes that there was some flexibility regarding the duty assignments from one organization to the next, so there may have been a variance of positions with this crew had they made it to the warfront.

The Shepard family kept all the letters Lewis sent home, along with a variety of other documents. In two letters to his mother, Lewis asked her to send any extra no. 17 stamps from their ration books. No. 17 stamps were to be used to purchase mail-order shoes between February and June 1943. When Lewis got his shoes, he noted in his letter home that he had to pay fourteen dollars for them because they were of high quality, but he felt they were worth the expense because his other pair was falling apart. In a letter dated April 23, 1943, he wrote, "This week we are flying from midnight to 5:00 in the morning." This was two months prior to the crash date, and Lewis was just beginning to get flight time. He also noted that he was almost done with phase one of training and was looking forward to moving along to phase two.

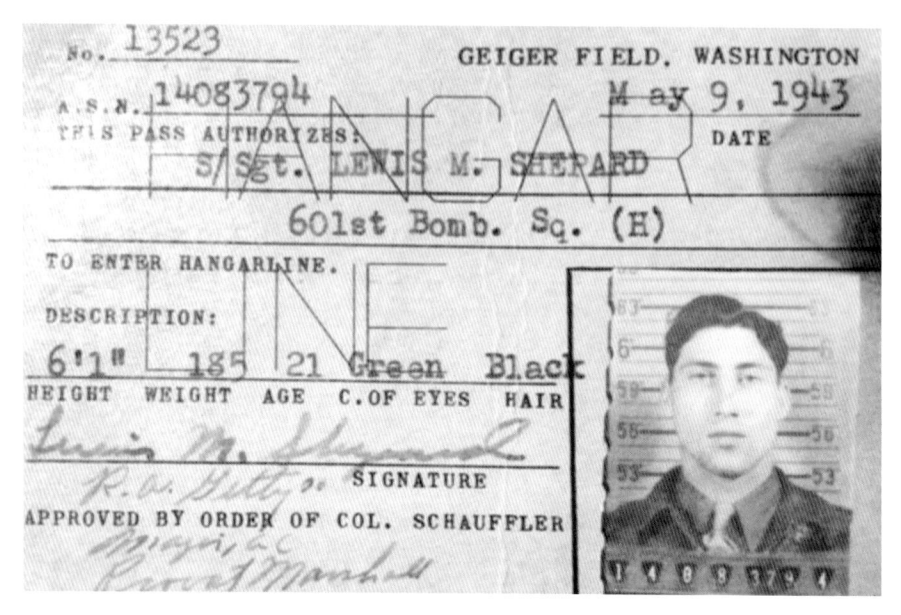

Lewis's military identification card. *Shepard family collection.*

By May 1, however, Lewis was trying to prepare his mother for his inevitable deployment. He could tell it was coming up sooner than expected, and he tried to reassure his mother that all would be well. He wrote:

> *Mama there is one thing that you will have to get used to & that is not hearing from me every week. Soon now it may be every month or even more because I only have two more here in the states & it may be that when I go across that we will not even be able to send out mail so if you do not hear from me for a while do not write to the commanding officer because most of the time he will not tell you a thing but just let me know that you wrote.*

Perhaps Lewis was anticipating what he thought would be an overreaction from a protective mother and was trying to avoid the future embarrassment of having his commanding officer tell him that his mother was calling to check on him. In this same letter, Lewis told his mother that he was going to begin his second phase of training, and that he was constantly tired because he was in training for more than sixteen hours a day.

A week later, Lewis found himself at Geiger Field in Spokane, Washington. He anticipated being there for a few months with his new squadron. That anticipated timeline was a bit off though, and by June 17, he again wrote home that he had been suddenly moved. This time, he was at the Walla Walla Army Air Base outside of Walla Walla, Washington. Things were speeding up, and he wrote his mother that he thought he would "go over much earlier than I expected because this is a third phase place." He was going to skip the second phase of training altogether.

Two of Lewis's brothers were in the service at this same time, and Lewis often asked about them in his letters. He expressed his hopes that neither Vernon nor Jack would be sent overseas to action. He penned, "I hope Vernon gets to stay in the States for the duration. I guess one of us over at the time is enough. I also hope something happens so Jack will not have to go." Lewis would never know that the war ended before Jack was deployed and that his unit was dissolved and he was sent home.

In what may have been his last letter home, dated June 26, Lewis told his mother that they would be leaving the United States very soon with one last stop before crossing the Atlantic. He believed they were going to England, and he included information that makes it clear that his crew was very newly formed and that he had not yet seen the *Scharazad*: "We will get our plane in a few days now. It will be a new one & one of the best out. There are lots of improvements on the new ones."

Lewis wrote some troubling things in his last letter home that either show a premonition of doom or perhaps that he was trying to reassure his mother about his safety in the war by taking the matter lightly.

> *As for me it does not matter. I was never any good any way always getting into trouble & causing you lots of it too. I am not worried about coming back. My pilot does not understand why I don't care while the rest of the boys on the crew are all worried about it. I could not tell him the truth so I just told him that there was no sense in worrying. I think he is glad that I am that way because it helps the rest of the crew. I guess there is not much more to say so until I can get a chance to write again. Don't worry about me. I am just not the type to get killed by a bullet. I will be hung yet. Love Lewis.*

Understandably, the loss of Lewis was difficult for his family. After two years of waiting while the crew was missing, they received notice on August 18, 1945, that Lewis's remains had been found at the crash site. The next day, they received another telegram notifying them that the remains were already being transported to Florida for burial.[181] This had to be a lot of emotionally charged information to handle in a short amount of time. Lewis

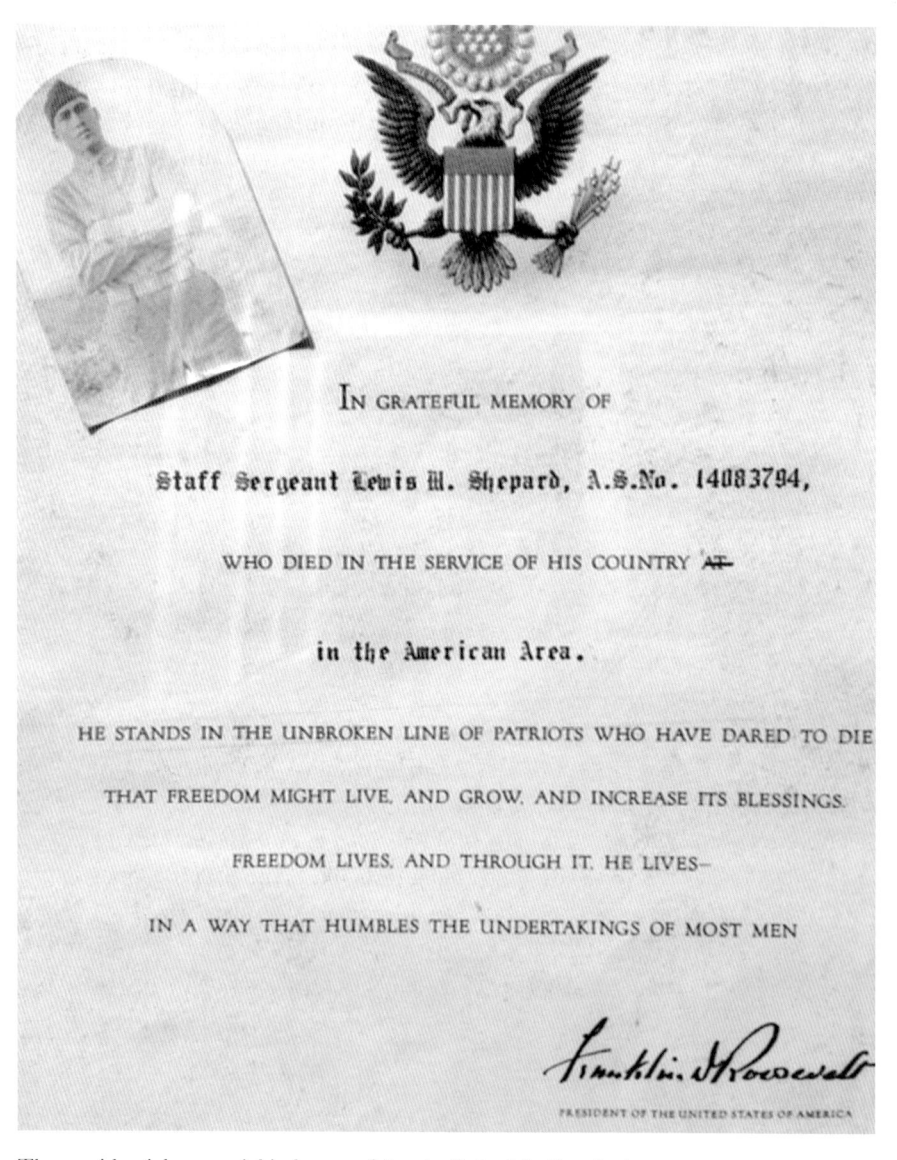

> IN GRATEFUL MEMORY OF
>
> Staff Sergeant Lewis M. Shepard, A.S.No. 14083794,
>
> WHO DIED IN THE SERVICE OF HIS COUNTRY ~~AT~~
>
> in the American Area.
>
> HE STANDS IN THE UNBROKEN LINE OF PATRIOTS WHO HAVE DARED TO DIE
>
> THAT FREEDOM MIGHT LIVE, AND GROW, AND INCREASE ITS BLESSINGS.
>
> FREEDOM LIVES, AND THROUGH IT, HE LIVES—
>
> IN A WAY THAT HUMBLES THE UNDERTAKINGS OF MOST MEN
>
> *Franklin D. Roosevelt*
> PRESIDENT OF THE UNITED STATES OF AMERICA

The presidential memorial in honor of Lewis. *Shepard family collection.*

was buried at the Evergreen Cemetery in Jacksonville, Florida. Later, his mother applied for a headstone from the military. On her application, she requested that the following information be included: Squadron H, 601st Bombardment Group, U.S. Army Air Forces. Officials who processed the application marked out some of this information, and a short memo that was attached was a query to determine if he was attached to that group and/or squadron. His name was also misspelled on the application, and his place of death was listed as the "Big Horn Mountains of Oregon."[182] It is easy to understand how these errors happened—but also how difficult they make later research.

Lewis's brother Jack visited Buffalo, Wyoming, and the area surrounding Bomber Mountain in later years. He and his wife, Geleeta, toured through the Bighorn Mountains and saw the beauty of the area, although Jack had a lingering wish to see the actual crash site.

The following are transcriptions of letters shared by the Shepard family:

Undated (Air Corps Technical School, Keesler Field, Mississippi letterhead)
Dear Mother,

I wrote you two letters and have not gotten an answer to either one of them. What is wrong at home, is everything all right, at least I hope it is. Last time I wrote I was in Camp Blanding now I am several thousand miles west and may go farther yet.

I won't hear for a week or so just when I will go. I have been taking lots of tests and exams for different jobs in the Air Corp [sic]. *I will be sent to some school I am sure but not sure where. If you write to Vernon soon give him my address and tell him to write me.*

By the way, I will be in close [sic] *something you can use in case I go with the war* [illegible word here, but it looks like "June"] *and not come back, I made out an insurance policy for $5,000 to you. It's paid out of my pay every month so I am not worrying about it not being paid.*

In case you will not get it all at once but in monthly allowances. I guess you will get a copy of the policy.

Write soon,
Lewis

My address now is
Pvt. Lewis M. Shepard.
1.SS. 309 Flt. 548
Keesler Field, Mississippi

· · · · · ·

(Undated)
Dear Mother,

I am sorry that I have not written to you sooner. I guess that I have been too busy to think of much but my school work. I am at the Armament School at Denver, Colo. I like it here lots although it is rather cold as we are right next to the mountains. I can see them all around us. Pikes Peak is very plain as is a lot [of] others. The air here is thin because we are so high up.

Most of the men here are either college men and had a couple of years at least. So that made it necessary for me to study an awful lot in order to keep up. You said that you had not heard from Vernon lately. Where is he now or do you know?

I got a letter from Jack, I guess he is home by now.

Well tell all the kids hello and write again soon.

As ever,
Your son,
Lewis

My new address is
Pvt. Lewis M. Shepard
21st Tech. Sch. Squadron (Spec)
Barrack #916
Lowry Field #2
Denver, Colo.

· · · · · ·

Undated (Air Corps Technical School, Keesler Field, Mississippi letterhead)
Mother,

I guess you are kinda surprised to hear from me here in Texas. I left Lowry Field last Monday. I got here today Thursday. I believe it is going to be swell here. The weather is rather warm. We are only 30 miles from the Mexican border.

We won't to be able to get out as often as we did at Lowry Field. We get off on Saturday evening and Sunday. I was hoping that it would be Florida that I was sent to. The bunch just before me was called out for Ft. Meyers. Just four men ahead of me they quit.

Well at least we got out of the cold weather. It was just beginning to get cold when we left.

I will be here for at least 5 weeks. I don't know just where I will be sent to I only hope I get a chance to come home before I go over seas [sic]. *Maybe after I finish this school I will get sent to the east coast.*

Did you get the diploma that I sent last week? That was for finishing armament school.

I will write again when I hear from you.

Your Son Lewis

· · · · · ·

Undated (HAGS Harlingen, Texas [all crossed out] *letterhead)*
Dear Mother,

I got your letter today. It followed me here to Salt Lake City so is a little late.

I am a Staff Sgt. Now, also an aerial gunner. I will be here for just a few days more.

I put in for the allotment for you at Camp Blanding. I thought you were getting it until you told me different. I will check up on it at once. If things get too bad before it is straightened out please let me know at once by Telegram. There is the emergency relief for soldiers I can always get them to see after you until the allotment is taken care of. The Red Cross will check on it so be sure it is on the level if you do wire me.

I will let you know when I get to my regular squadron. I will be here for a few days only so do not write here unless it is very necessary and if it is don't stop for anything let me know by wire so I can let the Red Cross take care of it.

It is cold up here.
Love,
Lewis

· · · · · ·

4/15/43
Dear Mother,

I got your letter yesterday, it was good to hear from you again. I also got a letter from Jack. I guess you have by now yourself.

I don't think that I will be here so very much longer about 3 weeks or more not more than 1 month.

We really start flying tomorrow in earnest. So far we have just been up a few times at nite [sic]*.*

If gossip is true we will be able to get 15 days off in about 3 months. I hope so for I would like to come home for a little while before I go across. You have not said anything about Dad lately, is he home? I believe he should be about now; is he?

I got a letter from Mr. Major and also Mr. Lewis. I am about to change my mind about Cadet. If I take it, it will mean 8 or ten months more of school and I have already had 6 mo. of it and have 3 more to go.

By the way, how many sugar books do you have, all of them. If you have enough #17 stamps will you send me one so I can get a pair of low cut shoes. I have one pair but they are about worn out and I would like to get another for dress. I hope we soon change to summer dress. This is one of the hottest and dustiest places I have ever been. It is [a] *lot hotter here than Fla. Even now in spring it is hotter than it is in Fla in the summer.*

They are just leveling off a field here next to my hut and every time a car goes by or there is a slight wind the dust goes up in a cloud. We never can keep anything clean.

Well I guess I will close for awhile [sic]*. If you have enough will you send me the #17 stamp.*

Love,
Lewis

· · · · · ·

April 23, 1943 (no letterhead)
Dear Mother,

I got your letter today. It is good to hear from you again. I thought that I answered all of your letters but maybe not. I have got 8 more days of training in my last phase here and hope to leave by the first of the month.

I am sorry to hear about dad. I was hoping that when he got out he would be better. I guess there is no hope of it though.

Thanks for the stamp. I can sure use it. My pair of shoes that I have now is about gone.

I got a letter from Jack yesterday. I will write him after I finish yours.

Up here now the wind is really blowing and the dust is so thick that you almost have to feel your way around. This week we are flying from midnight to 5:00 in the morning. Last night we were grounded because of bad weather. If it keeps up tonight like it has been all day I guess we will be tonight also.

By the time you get this I will have changed hours again. I will be flying in the morning from 6 till 11 and go to school in the afternoon.

Mama do you have a picture of Jimmy [Lewis's nephew], *if so send me one of him. As soon as they get some film, around here I will send you some of my self.*

I don't have too much of an idea as to where my next base will be but as soon as I get there I will let you know.

Well everything up here is about the same as ever so I guess I will close until I hear from you.

Love,
Lewis

· · · · · ·

May 1, 1943 (Army Air Base, Ephrata, Washington letterhead)
Dear Mother,

I got your letter, it was good to hear from you once more. I was glad to get the picture of Jimmy. He really looks swell. I would like to see him again.

I got my shoes with the stamp you sent to me. I got a really good pair. I paid $14.00 for them so they would last for a while. Mama there is one thing that you will have to get used to and that's not hearing from me every week. Soon now it may be every month or even more because I only have two more here in the states and it may be that when I go across that we will not even be able to send out mail so if you do not hear from me for a while do not write to the commanding officer because most of the time he will not tell you a thing but just let me know that you wrote.

I will still write to you as often as I can but working 16 hours a day here you are so glad to get to bed with out [sic] *worrying about writing letters. I guess by the time you get this I will be in my second Phase. I do not know where I will be yet but will let you know as soon as I get there.*

Love,
Lewis

• • • • • •

May 9, 1943 (Service Men's Center, 820 West Sprague Avenue, Spokane, Washington letterhead)
Dear Mother,

Well I have been moved again. I am now at Geiger Field in Spokane, Wash.

I hope I will be here for a few months yet. My squadron is a new one so I guess maybe I will.

I am sorry that I did not answer your letter before this but moving and everything. You know how it is.

You wrote to ask me about the allotment well I ask[ed] *about it and found out that a Staff Sgt. cannot get one but I may be able to get a Quarter Payment as it is called. I am going to try anyway.*

Is dad doing any better yet? I sure hope so. How is every one [sic] *at home yet?*

Did you hear from Vernon? I don't think Jack answered my last letter.

Boy you should see the sailors here in Spokane it is really bad. I came to town last night and was it crowded. I am not doing such a good job of writing this letter so I guess I will close until I get back to the base.

• • • • • •

Undated (318th Bombardment Squadron letterhead)
Dear Mother

I am sorry that I have not written to you before this but I have been awful busy. I had seven days off. I tried to get a plane home but I could not. So I went up to Lake Chelan a few hundred miles from here. I got a letter from Jack but have not answered it yet. I will after I finish yours.

Since I have been back I have not had time for hardly any thing [sic]. *We have just a few weeks more left now and I will be glad when we leave. I am sure tired of school.*

Has Vernon gone over yet, have you heard from him?

Well I guess there is not much more to say so I will close until I hear from you.

Love,
Lewis

. . . . . .

Undated (Walla Walla Army Air Base, Walla Walla, Washington letterhead)
Dear Mother,

Well I have been moved again. This time all of a sudden like. I am now in Walla Walla, Wash. About 170 miles from Spokane. I guess I will go over much earlier than I expected because this is a third phase base. We are skipping second phase of training.

Did you get the letter that I wrote to you from Geiger Field, did you answer it? I guess it will be sent on to me. This seems to be a nice place and I think I will like it.

I have not heard from Jack lately is he still at Camp Robinson? Tell him to write to me soon. I wish I could think of more to write but there is just nothing. Maybe when I get my next letter from you I can make my next one to you much longer. Have you heard from Vernon or Trish? If you write to Trish, tell her to write to me again.

Well until I hear from you again. So long.

Love,
Lewis
S/Sgt. Lewis M. Shepard
88th Bomb Grp (H)
318th Bomb Sqdn.
AAB Walla Walla, Wash.

. . . . . .

The Wyoming Bomber Crash of 1943

June 26, 1943
Dear Mother,

I have not heard from you in a couple of weeks. I hope you got my last letter.

Well it will not be long now by the time you get my next letter I will be heading out. I will have one more stop to make. It will be some place in Kansas. I will be glad when I get where I am going. From all that I can hear it will be England. I hope so. We will get our plane in a few days now. It will be a new one and one of the best out. There are lots of improvements in the new ones. I will call you before I leave the States.

Have you heard from Vernon or Jack lately? I hope Jack makes his cadet alright. If I had not of spent so much time in school I would have liked to go myself. When I get back I am going to put in for it. At least take up where I left off. I hope Vernon gets to stay in the states for the duration. I guess one of us over at the time is enough. I also hope something happens so Jack will not have to go.

As for me it does not matter. I was never any good any way. Always getting into trouble and causing you lots of it too. I am not worried about coming back. My pilot does not understand why I don't care while the rest of the boys on the crew are all worried about it. I could not tell him the truth so I just told him that there was no sense in worrying. I think he is glad that I am that way because it helps the rest of the crew.

I guess there is not much more to say so until I can get a chance to write again. Don't worry about me. I am just not the type to get killed by a bullet. I will be hung yet.

Love,
Lewis

12

MISSING

When the *Scharazad* and its crew failed to arrive in Grand Island, Nebraska, that event—or lack thereof—was immediately noted. The aircraft was reported as missing on June 29, 1943.

The *Scharazad*, piloted by William Ronaghan, had arrived at Pendleton Field on the afternoon of June 28. A few hours later, they were cleared for a formation takeoff with another B-17 when they left Pendleton Field, but for some reason, they did not do this and instead left minutes after the other aircraft and never caught up. That aircraft crew reported favorable weather and conditions for the duration of the flight and successfully landed at Grand Island. *Scharazad* was recorded as departing Pendleton Field at 8:52 p.m. PST with an expected flight duration of about six hours, which should have put them at their Nebraskan destination around 5:00 a.m. CST and likely put the time of the crash close to midnight.[183]

Although the fact that the aircraft was missing was not widely publicized to the general public, the U.S. Army took its disappearance seriously and immediately sent out search parties.[184] One search was conducted by personnel from the Casper Army Air Base from June 29 to July 5, 1943.[185] The report from July 9 noted that the "search [was] discontinued. No trace of plane or crew was observed in spite of favorable searching weather." The search missions were difficult, as there was a vast area to cover, and although an intact B-17 might be seen relatively easily from the air, one that has been broken into a million pieces is not.[186]

It is easy to imagine the heartache of having a loved one go missing. Certainly, parents, spouses and siblings felt the absence of their relatives keenly, but they also felt the absence of information.

About a month after the crew left Pendleton Field, Oregon, one of Pilot William Ronaghan's brothers received the following response to his query:

Provisional Group Detachment, 541st Bomb Squadron, 383rd Bombardment Group, Pendleton Field, Oregon
July 25th, 1949
Dear Mr. Ronaghan,

We are in receipt of your wire of July 22nd requesting information concerning your brother, 2nd Lt. William Ronaghan, missing in a plane that left Pendleton Field Oregon June 28th for Grand Island, Nebraska.

We regret that at the present time, there is no additional information to send you. There has been no trace of the plane since it left here.

Upon receipt of any information, you will be notified either by the Group or by the War Department direct.

For the Commanding Officer
Richard S. Nutt
2nd Lt., Air Corps
Adjutant

As each family grappled with the disappearance of their relative, they all sent inquiries and hoped for a positive outcome. In New York, the family and friends of Pilot William Ronaghan held a mass for his safe return at St. Francis Xavier Roman Catholic Church, which was located on the same street as the Ronaghan family home.

Within Leonard Phillips's military records are copies of letters from his mother, Libby, asking about the fate of her son. They are purely heartbreaking:

War Dept. Washington, DC. (received September 27, 1943)
Dear Sirs:

I would like some information about my Son 2nd Lt. Leonard H. Phillips, that was aboard a plane leaving Pendleton Field, Ore., June 28, 43.

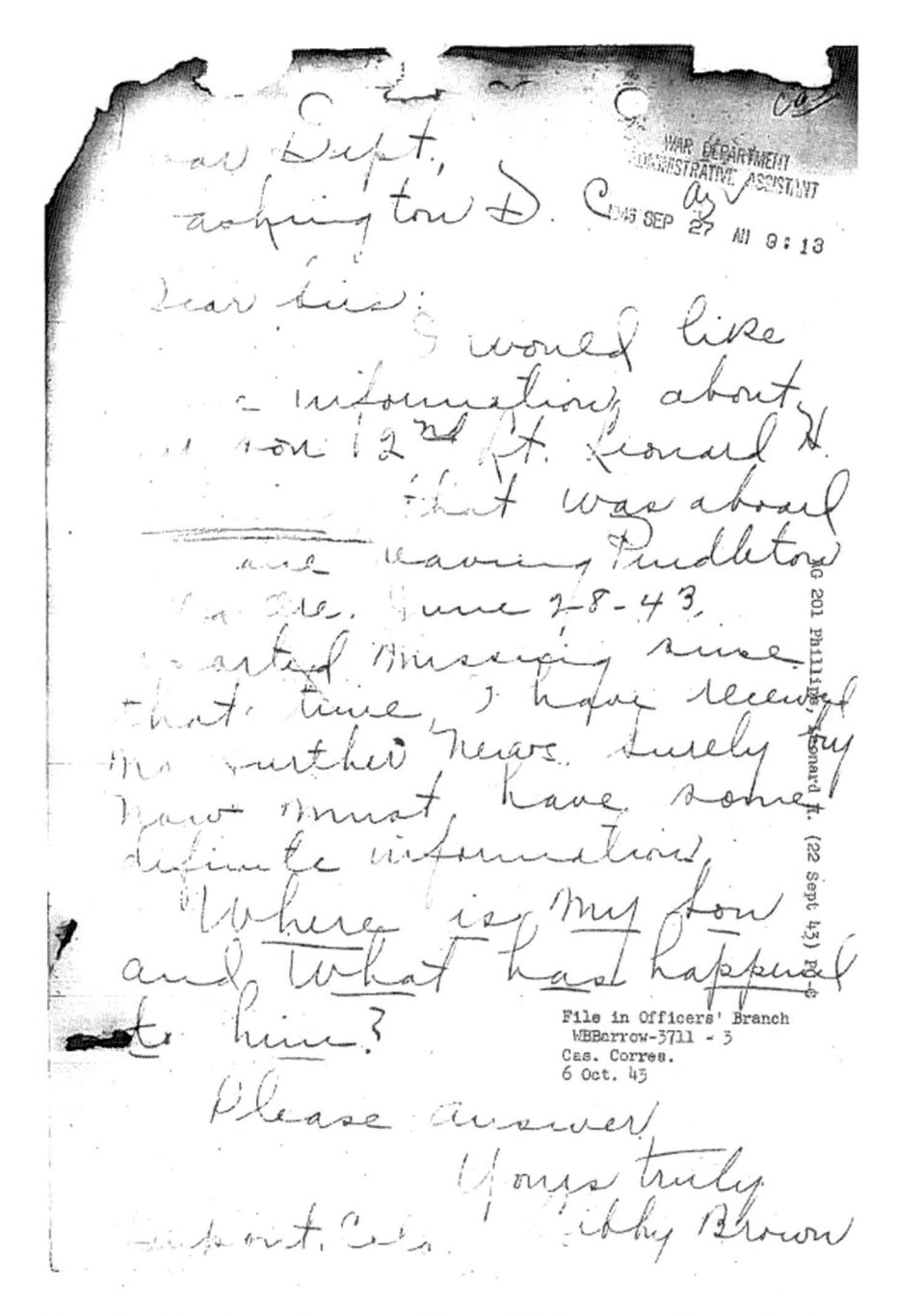

A letter from Libby Brown, the mother of Leonard Phillips. *National Personnel Records Center Collection.*

Reported missing since that time, I have received no further news. Surely by now [you] must have some definite information.
   Where is my Son and what has happened to him?

Please answer.
Yours truly,
Libby Brown
Dupont, Colo.

A response to Libby's plea came a few weeks later but was still not helpful:

Mrs. Libby Brown, Dupont, Colorado
Dear Mrs. Brown:

I have your letter of recent date in which your [sic] request information relative to your son, Second Lieutenant Leonard H. Phillips, who has been missing since 28 June 1943.
   I regret that up to the present time it has not been possible to obtain definite information regarding the circumstances surrounding the disappearance of your son. The military authorities are continuing their investigation, however, in an effort to ascertain his status and you may be certain that as soon as any further details are received, you will be notified promptly.
   My sincere sympathy is with you during this long period of uncertainty.

Very truly yours,
Lewis A. Hasty
Captain, A.G.D.
(from the office of J.A. Ulio, Major General, the Adjutant General)

Another letter from Libby Brown was sent off in February 1944, when she still had not received any useful information.

Dear Sir.

Several months ago, I had written to you, inquiring as to the whereabouts of my son, 2nd Lt. Leonard H. Phillips, reported missing since June 28.
   Your reply was no definite information. Surely by now, you must [have] some concrete information that I am allowed to know. I would much

AG 201 Phillips, Leonard H.
(28 Feb 44) PC-G O-678761

9 March 1944.

Mrs. Libby Brown,

    Dupont, Colorado.

Dear Mrs. Brown:

    Reference is made to your letter of recent date in which you request information relative to your son, Second Lieutenant Leonard H. Phillips, who has been missing since 28 June 1943.

    It is regretted that no information has reached the War Department relative to your son other than that contained in previous communications; however, a special effort is being made at this time to assemble and review all possible information pertaining to the disappearance of Lieutenant Phillips and as soon as this has been completed you will be advised of the determination made in the event it results in an official change of status.

    It is my hope that a favorable report will be received.

                  Sincerely yours,

                    J. A. ULIO
                  Major General,
              The Adjutant General.

A response letter to Libby Brown. *National Personnel Records Center Collection.*

rather have the hard cruel facts than this horrible silence. I have imagined everything and all of it bad.

I love him so very much, he is my only child and all I have. Please. Where is Leonard and what has happened to him?

Yours truly,
Libby Brown

Billy Ronaghan's mother sent a query around the same time.

March 2, 1945, Army Service Forces, Office of the Quartermaster General, Washington, D.C. Quartermaster General, Dear Sir,

On Nov. 20, 1944 I wrote for some information concerning my son's belongings to-day I receive a letter from Captain F.A. Eckhardt, Q.M.G. Assistant that he has no information of my son's things. Some one [sic] should know weather [sic] the boy took his things with him or not. I suppose his locker and things have been divided among some others. Kindly see if you can locate them. It sure does not look very good for this country to loose [sic] 10 men and a plane without a single trace [of] them.

Lt. William R. Ronaghan, 318 Squadron, 88 Bombardment Group, Walla Walla, Washington.

He left Pendleton Field, Oregon on June 28, 1943 for a new assignment at Grand Island, Nebraska and no information I receive has never been seen or heard of since.

Sincerely, (Mrs.) Mary Ronaghan, 1661 Lurting Ave., Bronx, NY 61

As time dragged on, these families had to turn their attentions to other tasks, like tying up financial and legal matters. A September 27, 1943 letter from Jefferson Standard Life Insurance Company to the Casualty Branch at the Adjutant General's Office asked the military to provide a certificate of death for Leonard Phillips, if possible, as the company had been contacted by his grandmother Frances Caldwell asking about settlement. The manager for Jefferson Standard noted that Phillips's premiums were being paid through the army payroll deduction plan.

By 1944, nobody believed the crew was still alive, but they needed answers and closure. The military declared the crewmen were dead one year after they went missing so that insurance policies could be settled and marital statuses sorted.[187] Family members were still searching for the men, but now, they also wanted the men's personal belongings returned.

Libby Brown received another letter from Major J.A. Ulio's office, dated July 4, 1944.

Dear Mrs. Brown:

Since your son, Second Lieutenant Leonard H. Phillips, 0-678761, Air Corps, was reported missing 29 June 1943, the War Department has entertained the hope that he survived and that information would be revealed dispelling the uncertainty surrounding his absence. However, as in many cases, the conditions of warfare deny us such information. The record concerning your son shows that he was a crew member of an airplane which departed from Pendleton Field, Oregon to a new station at Grand Island, Nebraska and failed to arrive at its destination. The airplane was last contacted over central Wyoming about midnight on 28 June 1943 and it has been found that he became missing on 29 June 1943 rather than the date first reported. Intensive search has failed to reveal any trace of the airplane or its crew.

Full consideration has recently been given to all available information bearing on the absence of your son, including all records, reports and circumstances. These have been carefully reviewed and considered. In view of the fact that twelve months have now expired without the receipt of evidence to support a continued presumption of survival, the War Department must terminate such absence by a presumptive finding of death. Accordingly, an official finding of death has been recorded under the provisions of Public Law 490, 77th Congress, approved March 7, 1942, as amended by Public Law 848, 77th Congress, approved December 24, 1942.

The finding does not establish an actual or probable date of death; however, as required by law, it includes a presumptive date of death for the termination of pay and allowances, settlement of accounts and payment of death gratuities. In the case of your son this date has been set as 30 June 1944, the day following the expiration of twelve months' absence.

I regret the necessity for this message but trust that the ending of a long period of uncertainty may give at least some small measure of consolation. I hope you may find sustaining comfort in the thought that the uncertainty with which war has surrounded the absence of your son has enhanced the honor of his service to his country and of his sacrifice.

Sincerely yours, David P. Richardson, Capt., A.G.D.

The following is a letter from Pilot Ronaghan's mother, Mary Ronaghan.

Sept. 25, 1944, Commanding Officer, 318 Squadron, 88 Bomb Group, Walla Walla, Washington.
Dear Sir,

Received the final notice of my son William R. Ronaghan who's last address above and his no was P.C.-G. 0-795445. Will you kindly send me his belongings such as his foot locker [sic] or anything else he had left behind him. Thank you.

Sincerely yours, Mary Ronaghan, 1661 Lurting Ave., Bronx, NY 61

Then came a response letter from Mayo A. Darling, quartermaster general assistant:

19 October 1944. Mrs. Mary Ronaghan, 1661 Lurting Avenue, Bronx 61, New York.
Dear Mrs. Ronaghan:

Your letter dated 25 September 1944 addressed to the Commanding Officer, 318th Squadron, 88th Bombardment Group, Walla Walla, Washington, has been forwarded to this office for necessary action in connection with the personal effects of your son, Second Lieutenant William R. Ronaghan.

A copy of your letter has been forwarded to the Effects Quartermaster, Army Effects Bureau, Kansas City Quartermaster Depot, 601 Hardesty Avenue, Kansas City 1, Missouri, for reply to you. That office has jurisdiction over the disposal of the personal effects of our military personnel outside the United States. If a reply is not received within a reasonable length of time, this office should be advised.

I extend to you my sincere sympathy in the loss of your son. For the Quartermaster General:

Sincerely yours,
Mayo A. Darling, Lt. Colonel, Q.M.C. Assistant

Then another letter was sent from Mayo A. Darling, quartermaster general assistant, to Mary Ronaghan:

24 March 1945. Mrs. Mary Ronaghan, 1661 Lurting Avenue, Bronx 61, New York.
Dear Mrs. Ronaghan:

Acknowledgment is made of your letter of recent date relative to the personal effects of your son, the late Second Lieutenant William R. Ronaghan.

It is believed that all of your son's personal effects were undoubtedly with him on the plane when he was lost. However, if you will contact the Summary Court Officer where he was last stationed information can be furnished you as to whether or not any of his personal effects were left there.

For the Quartermaster General:
Sincerely yours,
Mayo A. Darling, Lt. Colonel, QMC Assistant

Family members first grappled with the disappearance of their sons, husbands and brothers and then dealt with all of the paperwork involved when the men were declared dead by the military in July 1944 after a year's absence. Surely this absence was already deeply felt by all the families without the necessity of such an official reminder, but the official documentation was necessary for the families to receive benefits.

A year later, when the crews' remains were found, the families again had to deal with a new round of paperwork, rectifying the official dates of death.

13

FOUND

The *Scharazad* was certainly off-course. According to the last received radio transmissions from the aircraft, it should have been near the Powder River radio signal or closer to the town of Casper than it was to the Bighorn Mountains that tower over Buffalo. A statement from officials at Pendleton Field noted, "Two widely divergent position reports were received from Lt. Ronaghan, but these were the last heard from him as far as this office is concerned."[188]

Weather conditions could have been at play and perhaps contributed to the accident, but they do not seem to have been severe enough to have been the cause. Although the other aircrew who flew to Grand Island experienced good weather, it is possible the *Scharazad* ran into a storm system the others did not, as the two planes were obviously on different flight paths. Bernard H. Cooper, second lieutenant, air corps, weather officer, noted in the accident report, "It is possible that the aircraft encountered a thunderstorm, which are likely to build up over that area in the summer evenings, and the turbulence threw the aircraft down and into the top of the peak."[189] However, his official statement was a bit more complex when he noted that the northwestern section of the United States was experiencing a dome of polar air and stated, "No precipitation was encountered except for light sprinkling from dissipating afternoon cumulonimbus clouds over the 13,000-ft peak near Sheridan, Wyo. Visibilies were above 8 miles with no obstructions to vision having been reported."

Although it is far too easy to make judgements on past events, it is clear the *Scharazad* was drastically off-course and that this was the root cause of the crash. But at whose feet does the blame lie? The pilot's? The navigator's? Or perhaps the U.S. military was to blame, as it was churning out fresh-faced crews who simply did not have the experience and training necessary to make a six-hour flight in a noncombat zone. The latter seems the most logical when you remember that some airmen were given orders to skip entire phases of training.[190]

Although it is doubtful we will ever know exactly what happened in the moments leading up to the crash, one local man, Jim Davis, offered an insightful recollection of his visit to the site at the time of its discovery during a personal interview with the author.

Jim shared that on August 10 or August 11, 1945, when the wreckage was found, it was spotted by a large party of men. At least twelve men and teenage boys were in the area gathering cattle; they were all members of the Paint Rock Cattle Association, and they were conducting a roundup of the cattle that had been grazing in the mountains. Jim remembered everybody riding along the trail when a part of the aircraft came into sight directly in front of them. It was the large stabilizer piece of the tail, resting on the western slope of the ridgeline. Berl Bader and Albert "Patcheye" Kirkpatrick were some of the first to climb the mountainside and discover the remains of the crew. Other members of the party later climbed the mountain in small groups, while Bader and Kirkpatrick rode about five miles to the southwest to the Tyrell Ranger Station to report the crash to the U.S. forest ranger stationed there.

One of the men who visited the crash site was curious about the identities of the crew members and carefully moved the remains around, looking for dog tags or names printed on clothing. The others with him noted that he did not take anything from the men or the crash site but wanted to know more about the crew and was searching for identifying items. Keep in mind that these men were cowboys and more accustomed to dealing with death and gore than most.

There is a particular significance to this, as there has been a lingering idea that one of the crew members survived the initial crash and instead died alone of exposure. This thought was based on the recollections of others who also saw the wreckage before the military investigatory/recovery crew removed the remains; some claimed they saw the remains of one crew member leaned against a rock with some personal items placed around him. For decades, the idea that their loved one may have died a long, lonely death had haunted

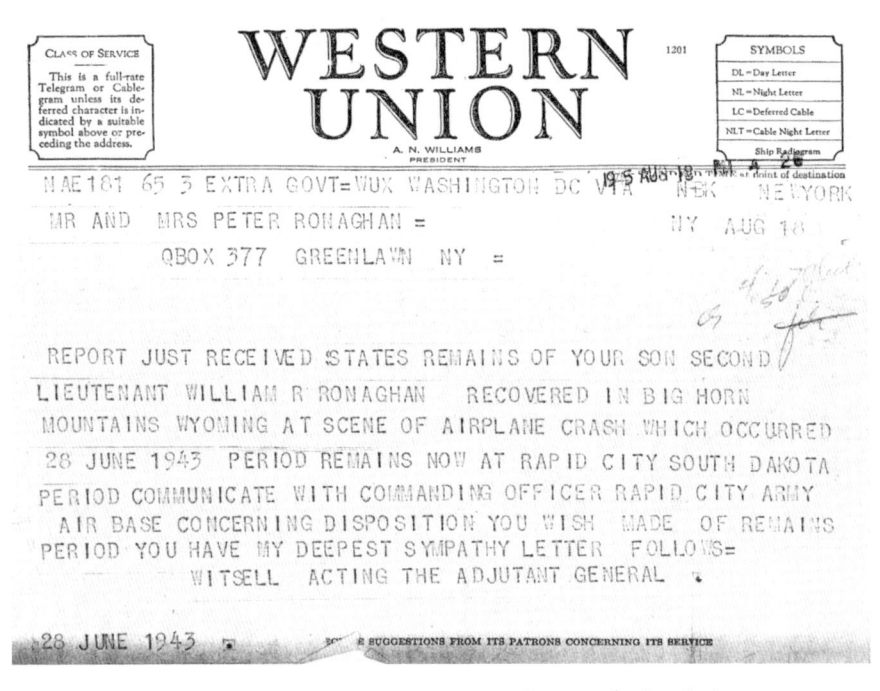

```
                                WESTERN                   1201
                                 UNION
                               A. N. WILLIAMS
                                 PRESIDENT
NAE181  65 3 EXTRA GOVT=WUX WASHINGTON DC VIA           NEW YORK
  MR AND    MRS PETER RONAGHAN =                  NY  AUG 18
        QBOX 377   GREENLAWN   NY =

  REPORT JUST RECEIVED STATES REMAINS OF YOUR SON SECOND
  LIEUTENANT WILLIAM R RONAGHAN   RECOVERED IN BIG HORN
  MOUNTAINS WYOMING AT SCENE OF AIRPLANE CRASH WHICH OCCURRED
  28 JUNE 1943  PERIOD REMAINS NOW AT RAPID CITY SOUTH DAKOTA
  PERIOD COMMUNICATE WITH COMMANDING OFFICER RAPID CITY ARMY
   AIR BASE CONCERNING DISPOSITION YOU WISH   MADE OF REMAINS
  PERIOD YOU HAVE MY DEEPEST SYMPATHY LETTER  FOLLOWS=
           WITSELL  ACTING THE ADJUTANT GENERAL .

 28 JUNE 1943
```

A telegram sent to William Ronaghan's mother, Mary. *Ronaghan family collection.*

many of the family members of the crew, but the most likely explanation is that in a cowboy's efforts to find identification, he unintentionally altered the scene, moving personal items and leaving the body in a propped-up position. It seems implausible that any small belongings survived the two years on top of the ridge without being blown away or disintegrating. With the benefit of retrospect, combining the memories of those who saw the site in the days during and after discovery of the crash offers the most sensible explanation of what happened.

As soon as employees of the U.S. Forest Service were aware of the crash site, they notified the U.S. military. By the night of August 11, an official recovery party was being organized.[191] The cowboys had found a roster of the crew at the wreckage, which they also provided to U.S. Forest Service Ranger Irving Massey, which explains how the aircraft and crew were identified so quickly before the recovery had even taken place.[192]

14

RECOVERY

Once word of the discovery was out, newspapers across the country picked up the story. Articles appeared in local papers but also from coast to coast with headlines like "Flyers Identified Who Died in Crash Two Years Ago," "10 Bodies Removed from Lost Fortress," and "Bodies Found High on Mountain Top."[193] Even though they all utilized a release from the Associated Press, many articles featured slightly different claims, with some being vastly inaccurate. The initial reporting said that six bodies were found.[194] Some claimed the crash site was located on Cloud Peak itself.[195] Many stated that the bodies were lowered by ropes.[196] And one claimed that Radio Operator Ferguson T. Bell "radioed a last message from an army plane as it was falling for a crash near Casper, Wyoming."[197] Others stated that the aircraft could not be identified as belonging to the military.[198] What is consistent throughout the reporting is the emphasis on noting that U.S. servicemen had been found, and they needed to be recovered.

Military personnel from Peterson Field, Colorado Springs, Colorado, and Rapid City Army Air Base, Rapid City, South Dakota, were immediately dispatched to organize the effort. Those from Colorado conducted an aerial sweep of the area, while the Rapid City crew was the ground party.[199] The investigation into the crash was led by Captain Kenneth G. Hamm. Accompanying Hamm up the mountain to the crash site was military photographer Private Charles Hylon Obert of Connecticut; medical officer Captain William Horton, MD,

Cover page of the 1945 accident report. Note the cause is listed as "undetermined." *Courtesy of the Air Force Historical Research Agency.*

of Newcastle, Wyoming; Special Investigator Tom Mathews; medical corpsmen Corporals Mayo B. Cantwell and Armand J. Romano; U.S. Forest Service Rangers Irving H. Massey and Urban "Herb" Post; Rapid City Army Air Base Commander Colonel William C. Lewis; cowboy and guide George McRae; and another guide named Bill (unfortunately Bill's last name is not noted).[200] Urban Post provided horses to ride and pack as well as supplies.[201] Apparently, the military personnel from Colorado did not partake in the recovery and instead returned to base.[202]

As the lead investigator, Hamm provided an official statement of witness as a part of the accident investigation:

> *I, Kenneth G. Hamm, Captain, Air Corps, 0-414799, assigned to Air Inspector Office, 354 AAFBU, Army Air Base, Rapid City, South Dakota, am a pilot on B-17 type aircraft. I have been a pilot of military aircraft for four years.*
>
> *Rapid City Army Air Base was notified at 2330, 11 August 1945, that a wrecked airplane had been found in the Big Horn Mountains, near Cloud Peak, approximately 18 miles NNE of Ten Sleep, Wyoming.*
>
> *On 14 August 1945, we approached to within two miles, on horseback, to the scene of the accident. We left the horses at Lake Florence, which was directly below the crashed airplane at an altitude of 11,900 feet. After proceeding to the airplane on foot, we noted that it had struck about 50 feet below the top edge of a saddleback ridge that rose gradually to the mountain peak, an altitude of about 13,000 feet. The altitude of the crash was about 12,800 feet.*
>
> *The pilot of the airplane, which we identified as a B-17, number 42-23399, had apparently seen the ridge at the last moment, attempted to pull up, and had hit the tail section first. The tail wheel and the rear part of the fuselage were on the west slope of the ridge. The airplane evidently struck the top of the ridge, depositing some debris, and then catapaulted [sic] over to the east slope of the ridge, where we found the main landing gear, parts of the wings, and radio room. The craft was totally demolished, and wreckage was strewn for approximately one-third of a mile. Parts of the airplane had burned, but it appeared that the disintegration had been so abrupt that those parts that did burn were not in any way connected with the rest of the airplane.*
>
> *The ridge was solid rock, and it was impossible to determine where any of the rocks had even been displaced by the impact.*

Left to right: Cantwell, Ranger Urban Post, Horton, Romano, Mathews, Hamm, Colonel William Lewis and George McRae at Hunter Ranger Station on August 15, 1945. *U.S. Army Air Corps.*

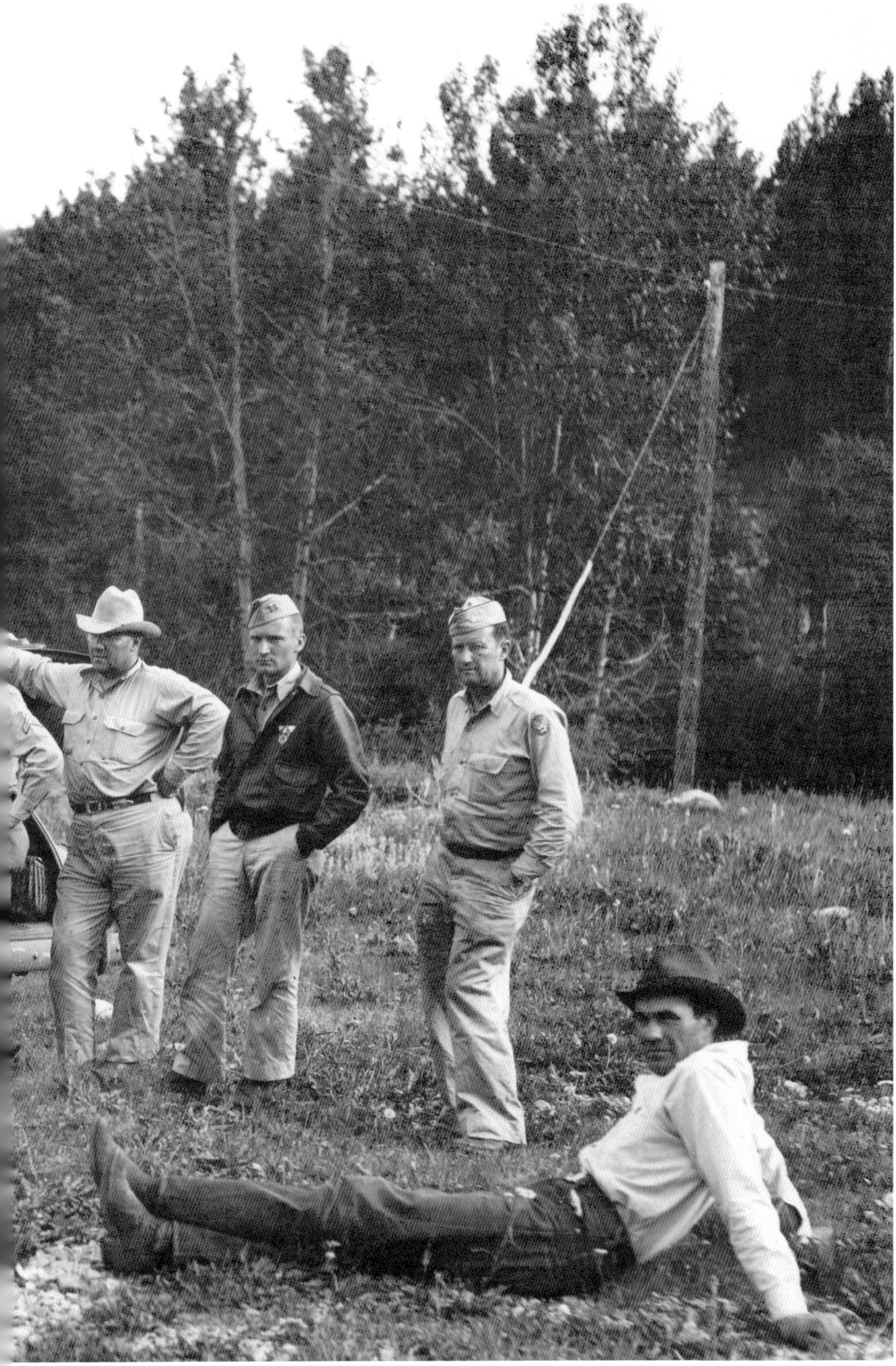

Organizing supplies at Hunter Ranger Station, August 13 or August 15, 1945. *United States Army Air Corps.*

Left to right: Corporals Cantwell and Romano, Captain Horton, Investigator Tom Mathews and Captain Kenneth Hamm at Hunter Ranger Station on August 15, 1945. *United States Army Air Corps.*

The Wyoming Bomber Crash of 1943

The compasses examined indicated they were on a heading between 150 and 170 degrees, as the magnetic compass was shattered at 170 and the directional gyro was jammed at 150 degrees.

Eight bodies were picked up on the west side and top of the ridge, and two picked up on the east side, all in advanced stages of decomposition. From their appearance, all had been killed instantly. One man still had an oxygen mask on, which indicated they may have been climbing to higher altitude at the time of the accident.

Because of the complete and utter destruction of the aircraft, we could not determine the condition of the engines at the time of the crash. Although some parts of the plane had burned, most of it had not, and many parts were wedged irretrieveably [sic] into the crevices in the rocks. Even parts of clothing were so tightly jammed between the cracks that they could not be extracted.

The crash occurred in such a place that it could not be seen unless one was at such an angle that he could see the sun flashing from the pieces of aluminum strewn about, and even then they could have been mistaken for snow, as there were several drifts about. During the winter, which was the greater part of the year, all of the wreckage would be completely covered by snow.

Image of the wreckage taken by Private Obert on August 14, 1945. *United States Army Air Corps.*

The Wyoming Bomber Crash of 1943

[Photograph of wreckage debris on rocky terrain, handwritten caption visible: "Crash At Cloud Mt Wyo June 1943"]

Opposite, top: Image of the wreckage taken on August 14, 1945. *United States Army Air Corps.*

Opposite, bottom: Close-up of a piece of wreckage debris taken on August 14, 1945. *United States Army Air Corps.*

Above: View of the debris on August 14, 1945. Oxygen tanks and one machine gun can be seen. *United States Army Air Corps.*

> *The bodies were all recovered, and taken to Rapid City. The airplane was left, as there was nothing salvageable.*
> *I have read the above and it is a true statement of what I saw.*
>
> Kenneth G. Hamm, Captain, Air Corps
> Witnessed by Robert V. Peterson, Capt, AC. Aircraft Accident Officer

Hamm's description of the accident was verified by members of the Accident Investigating Board, which included Colonel William C. Lewis, who was also present during the recovery mission.[203] Along with investigating the crash, Hamm was also tasked with recovering the bodies and determining whether a mission to remove any of the aircraft itself was worthwhile. Some of the information in the crash report is, quite bluntly, gruesome. At least four of the ten men were decapitated, and considering the noted lack of

The Wyoming Bomber Crash of 1943

Close-up of a piece of wreckage debris showing how the metal ripped and folded (August 14, 1945). *United States Army Air Corps.*

BC-375 high-frequency transmitter from the radio room, taken on August 14, 1945. *United States Army Air Corps.*

The Wyoming Bomber Crash of 1943

Close-up of a piece of wreckage debris taken on August 14, 1945. *United States Army Air Corps.*

Part of the debris field, with Special Investigator Tom Mathews visible at the top left (August 14, 1945). *United States Army Air Corps.*

AAF STATION HOSPITAL
RAPID CITY ARMY AIR BASE
Rapid City, South Dakota

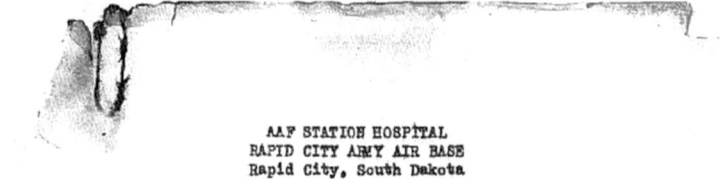

21 August 1945

1. ABSTRACT OF CLINICAL HISTORY:

   2d Lt. Leonard H. Phillips, 0678761, was one of the crew of a B-17 plane sailing from Pendleton Field, Oregon, to Grand Island, Nebraska, on 28 June 1943. All traces of the plane were lost on this date until the wreckage was discovered 16 August 1945, on Cloud Peak of the Big Horn Mountains, Johnson County, Wyoming. A detachment from the Rapid City Army Air Base reached the scene of disaster and found the entire crew of ten men dead. The bodies of the crew and wreckage of the plane were scattered over the glacier mountain peak for an area of about 400 yards, many of the bodies and parts of bodies were found wedged in between sharply pointed rocks. All of the bodies showed complete disintegration both from violence of the accident and the natural process of decay due to over two years exposure to the elements.

2. DESCRIPTION OF REMAINS OF 2d LT. LEONARD H. PHILLIPS, 0678761:

   This body showed complete disintegration with decapitation, there being only the torso remaining. The remains of this body consisted of a mass representing the torso measuring 12" x 12" x 30". There were no identification tags discovered on this body but identification was made by identifying papers on the clothing.

EDWARD D. MAIRE,
Major, MC,
Acting Base Surgeon.

Above: A Rapid City Army Air Base report regarding the remains of Navigator Leonard Phillips. *National Personnel Records Center.*

Opposite, top: Image of the debris taken on August 14, 1945. Pieces of the landing gear and engine are visible. *United States Army Air Corps.*

Opposite, bottom: Image of the aircraft tail taken on August 14, 1945. It shows the stinger style tail. *United States Army Air Corps.*

The Wyoming Bomber Crash of 1943

animal activity, the decapitation almost certainly occurred at the time of impact.[204] Once removed from the crash site, the men's remains were sent to be processed by the Campbell Funeral Home of Rapid City, South Dakota, in order to prepare them for shipment via railroad to their family members.[205] Documents from Campbell Funeral Home also corroborate the information in military records and Hamm's journal. Some bodies were noted to be in pieces and burned, all of which fits Hamm's description of there having been multiple fire spots at the crash site. Further information is contained in a letter from Lewis I. Horwitz:

Courts and Boards Office, Headquarters Rapid City Air Base, Rapid City, South Dakota. August 31, 1945.
Mrs. Peter Ronaghan, 1661 Lurting Avenue, Bronx, New York.
Dear Mrs. Ronaghan:

After returning to the Base here I made inquiry concerning those matters which you questioned me about when I visited you at your home. I spoke to the officers who brought your son's body from the mountain and I learned from them and from notes by them that identification was made by papers found in his clothing.

A wallet was found on your son, but the contents were partially burned. Apparently he had some money in the wallet, but the exact amount could not be ascertained because of the burned condition. The charred bills were sent to the Treasury Department in Washington in an effort to ascertain the amounts. When and if these amounts can be ascertained, the money will be forwarded to you.

The reason that you received no personal possessions at the time of your son's death was because the flight was made on a permanent change of station and he had all his possessions on the plane. The plane was scheduled to fly from Pendleton Field, Oregon, to Grand Island, Nebraska. One of the officers in the rescue party whom I questioned informed me that no effects could be salvaged from the wreckage.

I asked him in particular about whether or not a ring was found on your son's body and he informed me that no ring was found. The charm you mentioned to me was probably burned or otherwise lost.

If there are any questions you have or any other matters in which I can be of assistance to you, do not hesitate to call upon me.

Respectfully yours, Lewis I. Horwitz, Captain, Air Corps.

15

CAPTAIN KENNETH HAMM

While the accident report very clearly states that no one survived the crash, a person might argue that the official crash report was written with the intention of shining an undeserved positive light on the military by incorrectly indicating all the men had died immediately upon impact with no undue suffering. However, there is little evidence of this occurring, and there is no known reason for the person in charge of the accident investigation to hide or alter anything in his personal writings.

As noted in his witness statement, Captain Kenneth G. Hamm was also a B-17 pilot—and a well-traveled one at that. He piloted over fifty missions and was a lieutenant colonel when he was discharged from the military. He was with the Thirty-Second Bomb Group, Twelfth Air Force, and even flew a B-17 from Rapid City Air Base, South Dakota (now known as Ellsworth Air Force Base), to the town of Rock Springs, Wyoming, because a fellow military officer needed a ride to see his father in Evanston, and Rock Springs was the closest they could get with a B-17.[206]

After the war, Hamm returned home to Sweetwater County, Wyoming, and went on to become a district court judge of the Third

Captain Kenneth Hamm. *Judge Kenneth G. Hamm Collection, Rock Springs Historical Museum, Rock Springs, Wyoming.*

Hamm with *Leadfoot*, one B-17 he flew during World War II. *Judge Kenneth G. Hamm Collection, Rock Springs Historical Museum, Rock Springs Historical Museum, Rock Springs, Wyoming.*

Judicial District after practicing law for a number of years.[207] Hamm had a reputation throughout his life for being meticulous and detailed, and over the years, he amassed a large collection of his personal diaries. He also wrote a number of historical articles focusing on the people of Sweetwater County. What follows is an excerpt from his diary that covered the dates of the recovery and his experience:

August Thursday, 9–Thursday 30, 1945

From the 9th through the 11th, there was little to do except the same routine stuff. However, on the night of the 11th the base had a phone call from 2nd Air Force notifying them of a B-17 wreck that had been discovered on a mountain in Wyoming. Then about 8:00 AM on Sunday 12, I got a phone call from the staff duty officer telling me that Colonel Lewis was organizing [an] expedition to investigate the crash and brign [sic] down the bodies. I thought [he] was kidding, especially when he told me that the plane had been wrecked for two year [sic] and three months, as it had crashed on 28 June 1943. However, he assured me it was no gag, so I threw some things together as quickly as I could, came out to the base, waited for the colonel, and then drove his [car] back to town. Picked up a couple more things in the meantime and about 11 we started. Colonel Lewis drove a staff car and Pvt. Obert, the base photographer, and I rode with him. We got to Newcastle, Wyoming, fooled around there for a while, and picked up a couple of medical corpsmen named Cantwell and Romano who were over there taking care of military personnel during the rodeo. Captain Horton, the base surgeon was also there.

We left Newcastle with the staff car and an ambulance. In Gillette, we picked up another man named Tom Matthews, a special investigator for South Dakota. From there, Matthews, Horton, the Colonel and I all rode in the Staff [sic] car to Buffalo, Wyoming, and I listened to their bullshit all the way there. Tom Matthews could throw more bull faster and farther than any man I ever saw, and the Colonel ran him a close second. However, all was amicable and we had only a little trouble when the ambulance started to lose oil. We had no tools, and were out in the middle of the prairie when apparently out of nowhere appeared a little Swede who had ten years' experience with the Chrysler motor company. He fixed the leak in a flash, had a drink and we drove on.

Stayed in Buffalo all night and then on Monday 13th we drove on to the Hunter Ranger Station about 15 miles from Buffalo. There we arranged with the ranger to provide the horses, and pack our equipment and food to our camp site near the wreck. We proceeded on to the Meadowlark Lodge about 20 miles or more past the ranger station. There we met a couple of majors, a captain, and a private who had come from Colorado Springs to arrange for the trip. They didn't do anything and one of the majors, who was in charge, didn't even want to go up on the mountain so none of them went. We got our horses there, although we still had about fifteen miles to take the cars. Therefore, Captain Horton, the guide, whose name was Bill, Private Obert, and myself had to take the horses to the camp site. We each had to tow a horse as well. About the first mile, that damned horse nearly beat me to death, as I've never ridden before except once when I was five, and once for about half a mile on one of Ned Moerke's horses. It wasn't so bad when the horse walked, but when he started to trot, he slapped hell out of me. I decided about that time that I had better learn how to ride, and after trying for awhile [sic], didn't do so badly.

We rode horseback about 18 miles to our camp, and it took about 6 hours, as the trail disappeared where the beavers had dammed the creek, and we couldn't find the crossing. Finally discovered a way through the brush, and Captain Horton was jabbed with a broken branch that just missed his eye.

The Wyoming Bomber Crash of 1943

Meadow Lark Lodge with a military car and ambulance, August 13, 1945. *United States Army Air Corps.*

Where the horses were left while the men climbed the mountain during recovery on August 14, 1945. *United States Army Air Corps Image.*

Above: Bomber Mountain with Mistymoon Lake below, August 8, 2014. *Author's collection.*

Right: An oil painting of Suppie, done posthumously by artist Loris Withers. *Image courtesy of Kelsey McDonnell.*

Suppie sent this nose art–style drawing to "Uncle Bob and Aunt Gertrude." *Suppes family collection.*

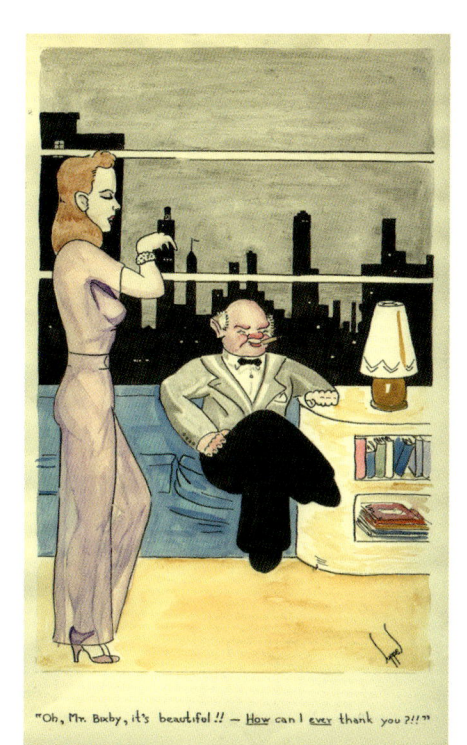

Left: Although the innuendo is obvious, it is unknown if Suppie created this from a lived experience or was referencing pop culture. *Suppes family collection.*

Below: Remnants of an oxygen tank, August 9, 2014. *Author's collection.*

Crushed metal in the debris field, August 9, 2014. *Author's collection.*

A piece of crumpled metal wedged in boulders, August 9, 2014. *Author's collection.*

Debris in the rocks on a steep incline, August 9, 2014. *Author's collection.*

Pieces of debris showing rust and faded paint from exposure, August 9, 2014. *Author's collection.*

An engine oil cooler wedged beneath a boulder, August 9, 2014. *Author's collection.*

A portion of the debris field along the top of Bomber Mountain, August 9, 2014. *Author's collection.*

A view of various parts that have been separated and scattered, August 9, 2014. *Author's collection.*

A portion of the debris field going over to the east side of Bomber Mountain, August 9, 2014. *Author's collection.*

A wider view of pieces along the top of Bomber Mountain, August 9, 2014. *Author's collection.*

A small, mangled piece, August 9, 2014. *Author's collection.*

Part of the Dyna motor from the radio room, August 9, 2014. *Author's collection.*

A view showing the Dyna motor part in context of the scale of Bomber Mountain, August 9, 2014. *Author's collection.*

Possibly a part of a gun turret mechanism, August 9, 2014. *Author's collection.*

Debris, August 9, 2014. *Author's collection.*

Another piece of the Dyna motor from the radio room, August 9, 2014. *Author's collection.*

On top of Bomber Mountain looking toward Florence Pass, August 9, 2014. *Author's collection.*

Top: Another piece of one of the engine's turbochargers, August 9, 2014. *Author's collection.*

Bottom: Looking downhill at pieces of debris across the rock field, August 9, 2014. *Author's collection.*

Top: Remnants of the throttle quadrant control stand from the cockpit, August 9, 2014. *Author's collection.*

Bottom: Remnants of one of the front landing gear/wheels with the hub of the other in the background, August 9, 2014. *Author's collection.*

Pieces of an inflatable life vest, August 9, 2014. *Author's collection.*

A large piece of debris showing graffiti from site visitors, August 9, 2014. *Author's collection.*

A portion of the top of the aircraft that was behind the cockpit and held an emergency life raft, August 9, 2014. *Author's collection.*

Remnants of one of the four Wright Cyclone engines, August 9, 2014. *Author's collection.*

Image of the tail stabilizer, August 9, 2014. *Author's collection.*

Image of the Sperry top turret with its parts stripped, August 9, 2014. *Author's collection.*

Where the horses were left while the men climbed the mountain during the recovery on August 14, 1945. *United States Army Air Corps.*

Reached Lake Helen about 8:00 at night and started camp. Before we got there, we had to stop at another lake about 8 miles back where the others left the cars and get them mounted. The country started getting rough about then. Our camp site was just about timberline, and it was a little cold. It also started to rain just as we pitched camp, got dark and miserable, and we hadn't had anything to eat. The first meal was not very good but it was welcome, and everyone turned in right afterward. Colonel Lewis did all the cooking, both for that meal and all subsequent meals. It stopped raining about ten and things were a little nicer. On the way from Rapid City, this Tom Matthews was telling what he was going to do, but when it came to carrying his own backpack, he flunked, and let one of the medical corpsmen and the guide carry it. During the night a brown bear invaded the camp but didn't disturb much. The beds got wet during the rain and some of the boys slept a little cold all night. The trip was too hastily prepared and we had insufficient tarpaulins and the food lacked variety. However, we didn't fare too badly.

The next morning, on Tuesday 14, we packed only the things we needed such as rubber sacks for the bodies, ropes, camera, etc., and rode another 6

The Wyoming Bomber Crash of 1943

This page and opposite: The campsite during the August 1945 recovery trip. *United States Army Air Corps.*

or 7 miles further up into the mountains to a Lake Florence. This lake was way above timberline, at an altitude of 11,900 feet. There were absolutely no trees at all, not even scrub pine. There we had to leave the horses, each of us who went up in the mountain took a rubber sack and some rope, and we started off individually, in twos, or threes, to make the climb. The terrain was extremely rugged—huge boulders, snow drifts, waterfalls, and sliding shale.

 A ranger named Massey and I were there first, and we had trouble finding the wreck for a few minutes. The plane was so completely demolished that we were almost on top of it before we saw it. I noticed that the plane had struck about 50 feet below the top edge of a saddleback ridge that rose gradually to the mountain peak. The wreck occurred at an altitude of about 13,000 feet. The pilot of the airplane, which we identified as a B-17, number 42,23399, had apparently seen the ridge at the last moment, attempted to pull up, and had hit the tail section first. The tail wheel and rear part of the fuselage were on the west slope of the ridge. The airplane then struck the top of the ridge, leaving some wreckage, and then catapaulted [sic] over to the east slope, where we found the main landing gear, parts of the wings, and radio room. The plane was totally demolished, and wreckage was strewn for approximately one-third of a mile. Parts of

The Wyoming Bomber Crash of 1943

An image of the packhorses at the base of what would become Bomber Mountain, August 14, 1945. *United States Army Air Corps.*

Captain Kenneth Hamm and Special Investigator Tom Mathews (*center*), August 14, 1945. *United States Army Air Corps.*

The Wyoming Bomber Crash of 1943

Special Investigator Tom Mathews at the base of what would become Bomber Mountain, August 14, 1945. *United States Army Air Corps.*

> *the airplane had burned, but it appeared that the disintegration had been so abrupt that those parts that did burn were not in any way connected with the rest of the airplane. The ridge was solid rock—just great boulders piled one on another with out [sic] any plan—and it was impossible to determine where any of those rocks had even been displaced by the impact.*
>
> *The compasses examined indicated they were on a heading between 150 and 170 degrees, as the magnetic compass was shattered at 170 degrees and the directional gyro jammed at 150. The scene of the accident was about 18 miles NNE of Tensleep, Wyoming, in the Big Horn Mountains, near Cloud Peak, and the plane was enroute from Pendleton, Oregon, to Grand Island, Nebraska, and was apparently slated for immediate overseas assignment.*
>
> *We picked up eight bodies on the west side and top of the ridge and two on the east side, all in advanced stages of decomposition. Under ordinary circumstances, at a lesser, warmer altitude, there probably would have been nothing left but bones, but the refrigerating effect of the climate kept them fairly well. Most of them were dismembered in one way or another, and*

all had been touched by fire. The first one was dried and parchment like. Some of the others were half bone, and the other half, which was protected by rocks and the fact that they were lying down, was still flesh and bone, crawling with maggots. We picked up arms, legs, and one pelvis lying loosely about. Ribs were scattered everywhere, and little slivers of bone. The identification was not so difficult as we thought it would be. Fortunately, some of them were wearing dog tags, and other [sic] *had some clothes on with identifications in their pockets. Massey, the ranger, couldn't smell so well, and he was invaluable during the process of identification. He would nonchalantly turn them over, dig in their pockets for identification, completely oblivious of the maggots crawling over his hands. We straightened them out as well as possible, put each of them into a rubber sack, except in case of those who were broken up so badly that we could put two in a sack, took pictures of the wreck, and then started down the mountain.*

I had a body that weighed about 80 pounds, a cowboy named George McRae had another of the same weight, one ranger had one about 50 pounds, Colonel Lewis and Massey had the last body we found, which was in the best state of preservation and weight [about] *100 pounds, Doc Horton was helping Lewis, and the one medical corpsmen had another about 80 pounds. However, by the time Horton got half way* [sic] *down the mountain, the medical corpsman came running down to him, and told him that the photographer had pooped out and couldn't go any further. The photographer was helping him. Horton then went back a ways and helped the corpsman, Romano, with the body. I carried my man all the way down and every step was agony. I had blisters on my toes, and after awhile* [sic] *it was all that I could do to lift him after a rest period. The cowboy and the ranger with me wre* [were] *also pooped out, but we kept going, and cursed every step of the way. Beyond doubt, it was one of the most torturous jobs I've ever undertaken, and about the last hundred hards* [yards] *of that two mile climb down was a rubber kneed stumble. All that got me in was sheer will not to quit. Everybody was so damned tired when we got down that they just flopped. Some left their cadavers about 100 yards from the camp and took the horses over to them, they were so tired. The weight of the bodies and roughness of the terrain, the distance, and the extreme altitude* [that] *created mild anoxia, all coupled with the fact that we hadn't eaten since breakfast made it a very miserable day. Then we had to ride horseback the seven miles back to camp.*

We left the bodies at Lake Florence to be picked up the next day by the rangers on their way back to their station. So I can truthfully say that at the instant the war was declared ended, I was staggering down a mountainside with a dead man on my shoulder. The men died instantly, fortunately for them. All their personal effects were so ruined by the weather and the crash that few of them were worth retrieving. Because of the complete and utter destruction of the aircraft, we could not determine the condition of the engines at the time of the crash. Although some parts of the airplane had burned, most of it had not, and many part [sic] were wedged irretrievable [sic] into crevices in the rocks. Even parts of clothing were so tightly jammed between the cracks that they could not be extracted. I took what little was left of their personal effects and stored it away for future reference. We ate at Lake Florence and no one had the least disinclination to eat. The sight of the bodies didn't bother any of us, but the smell was nauseating—even the doctor was caught short a couple of times. With the man on my shoulder and a small L-shaped tear in the sack, I got a blast of foul air every once in a while that damned near sent me to my knees.

Everybody hit the sack early and slept like logs. The next morning we packed up, rode back down the trail, doing a little fishin [sic] on the way. Our luck wasn't so good as we waited too long to start and it was in a place where people could come without too much trouble. Where we camped, on Lake Florence [he may have been referring to Lake Helen], we could pull fish out right and left but they were all too small to have any fun with. Just the right size for eting [sic] however.

Everybody stood the trip quite well, and Colonel Lewis, although 53 years old and the oldest man in the party, was about the most active. He went up the mountain with everyone else and worked hard all the time, even to doing the cooking. He was a little perturbred [sic] about Obert, the photographer who quit, and didn't care much for him after that. Obert, one of the biggest men in the outfit, just couldn't go another step, and sat down. He finally staggered down the hill though. Tom Matthews, despite his big talk, didn't do a damned thing except carry a little sack down the hill. Claimed his heart was bad, and I suppose it was as he wasn't exactly a young man.

Drove to Buffalo and spent the night there. Had a hell of a time getting a place to stay as everything was closed because the war was over. Finally routed out a secretary for one of the tourist lodges, and the enlisted men got the sheriff to open a restaurant for us. After a bath and a shave, we all felt a heck of a lot better. Went down to George McRae's for a few drinks and got a little high. The next morning we drove to Gillette and let Tom Matthews off, and then went on to Newcastle. Ate at Captain Horton's house, as he *lives in Newcastle, and left him there so he could accompany the bodies back to Rapid. The colonel and I came on home.*

From everything I heard, every town in the country had a big celebration the day the war ended, with people shouting, cars honking, and drinks flying all over the place. And I missed it. Four bloody years in the army and where am I—packing a dead man. And on the day it started where was I—a cadet confined to the post because they thought they might have to use us for the war at once.

16

BERL BADER

During the winter of 2018, this author was fortunate to meet descendants of Berl Bader, who shared family stories and information. Due to Bader's name being so strongly attached to the discovery of the crash site, some family members of the crew wrote to him personally. The following letter was from the mother of Ferguson Bell:

507 N. Holly Street
Little Rock, Arkansas
September 18, 1945
Dear Mr. Basten [sic]*:*

I am writing in regards to the Army plane you and your friend found on the slopes of Cloud's peak. I am Mrs. Frances Bell, Mother of S/Sgt. Ferguson T. Bell, whose body was found at the wreck.

I want to thank you and your friend for climbing the mountain and finding the plane and my son's body. You found the plane when all Army planes going over were not able to locate the wrecked plane and I am very grateful to you both.

I will never understand why the Government did not send out searchers on foot to find that plane, all the boys Mothers appealed to our Government to do so. I knew they would never find it flying over those mountains for I lived out there, at Riverton, Wyoming years ago and I knew how impossible it would be to locate a wrecked plane just flying over

Berl Bader. *Bader family collection.*

those mountains so you see it never would have been found if you had not climbed up and found it. Enclosed is a clipping and picture of my son, thought you would like to see it, he was my only child and his death has been very hard for me.

Col. Lewis of the 2nd Air Force of Rapid City, South Dakota, commanding officer who had charge of removing the bodies sent me a letter about the accident and gave me details but I would like for you to write me and give me more information please for the Col. had such a short time to write his letter in time to give it to the S/Sgt. who took my son's body home to give to me he failed to tell me several things I would like to know. The war being over now the Government doesn't care how much information I get concerning the accident—so please write me soon and tell me, it will help me to know more about it.

I understand there was only one body found with or near the tail of the plane and it was my sons. I was told the other nine boys went over the peak on the other side. [This conflicts with Hamm's report and diary.] *You reached the accident first, and was there just one body near the tail of the plane? My son had blond hair and weighed about 175 pounds. Col. Lewis took my boys tag off his neck, it had his name, serial number and my name and address on it, he also sent me my sons school ring with his initials on inside of the ring so I judged by that my boy's body was not broken up.*

I had a letter from Mr. and Mrs. F.G. Purcell of Buffalo, Wyoming (Mr. Purcell is a Jeweler there), stating they had a wrist watch [sic] *which was found at the accident and they thought it might be my sons they asked me to describe his watch but it had been so long since I had seen it I could not describe it. He did have his watch when he was home on furlough June 4th and 5th 1943, before he was lost June 28, 1943. Did you or your friend turn a watch in to Mr. Purcell and if so was it found near my son's body or on the side where his body was? I would like so much to have the watch to keep if it were his. Did you notice any of the boys' oversea bags near the plane? Was my son's body thrown clear of the plane a great distance or was it in the tail or near it? You may not think small things like that are very helpful but they are very near a Mother's heart and I would like to know everything. Were the boys' faces recognizable or too decomposed? Why were just six bodies given as found when there were ten on the plane? The Col. told me ten were found? Guess the others were under some of the wrecked plane. Were the boys' clothes on them or torn off? Please answer each question because I had rather know it all and it would help to set my mind at rest.*

Enclosed is a self addressed stamped envelope, will appreciate an answer as soon as possible.

Yours very truly,
Frances Bell
To
Mr. Berl Basten
Tensleep, Wyoming
September 18, 1945 at 10:30 am. Little Rock, Arkansas

The following is a letter Bader received from the parents of Charles "Junior" Newburn.

Wister, Okla.
Sept. 19th 1945
Mr. Berl Bader
Ten Sleep Wyo.
Dear Sir,

I have a clipping from our Daily paper that says you were one of the cowboys that found the plane wreck on Cloud Peak in which was found the body of our son S/Sgt Charles E. Newburn Jr. which had been lost 2 years June 28th.

We are very grateful to you & the other man in that we finally know what became of our Dear Boy although it is heartbreaking, as you must know, to think he had to lose his life in such manner.

We realize though that he might have suffered more had he gone on across.

Please write & tell us all you can about the finding & rescue if you get this. We don't know any street number or box number, just your town & name.

Our boy had my Electric Iron & several other keepsakes or would be if had them. Do you happen to know if they were found. They would be very sacred to us if we had anything of his he had. They sent us a few things that were in his billfold.

Please accept our thanks again and write to us. Also if you are ever down in this part of the country would be glad and really expect you to visit us.

Sincerely,
Mr. & Mrs. Charley E. Newburn
Wister, Okla.

P.S. we had a letter from Col. Lewis the man who helped in the rescue & sent us a picture of the scene made from an airplane. There's a man sitting there on a rock & we wonder if it is one of you men. He has on a Big Hat & a heavy coat.

To Berl Bader,
Ten Sleep
Wyoming

The Wyoming Bomber Crash of 1943

The following is from Vesta Wolfenbarger, the mother of James Hinds.

Sept. 12, 1945
Dear Mr. Bader,

I understand you were one of the men whom discovered the plane wreckage. I'm the mother of one of the Boys.

I wonder if you would mind describing it to me. Was it a complete crash or do you believe the boys lived awhile.

I know it must have been very rugged or would have been found sooner.

I have two more sons in the services. One in India now. The youngest is in Washington D.C. he spent thirty months over seas [sic]. I've been so alone since this war, but I do realise [sic] I'm just one mother. And some have lost all they have. My boys and I were very close their father having passed on when they were very small.

Thanking you in advance.

Sincerely,
Vesta Wolfenbarger
Sent via air mail. September 13, 1945, from Hermosa Beach, Calif. At 6 AM to Mr. Beryl Bader, Ten Sleep, Wyo.

Bader also received a letter from the air force.

Headquarters Second Air Force
Office of the Commanding General
Colorado Springs, Colorado
29 August 1945
Mr. Bert Baden [sic]
Buck Creek Cow Camp
c/o Mr. Irving H. Massey
U.S. Forest Ranger
Ten Sleep, Wyoming
Dear Mr. Baden:

I wish to commend you for your assistance to this headquarters in locating and identifying an airplane which crashed near Cloud Peak in the Big Horn Mountains of Wyoming.

You have in this instance rendered the Army Air Forces a definite service in a most difficult and hazardous mission, which reflects great credit to yourself.

I extend to you the highest commendation and the fullest appreciation of this command.

Yours truly,
Robert B. Williams
Major General, USA
Commanding

17
HONOR

It is an undeniable, cruel fact that these ten men died far too young. Thrown together to fight in a conflict far beyond their control, they had no opportunity to gain fame and respect like those who completed missions, earned medals and saw combat. You will not find the names of these ten men in the books and memorials of bomber groups, squadron histories or plaques and monuments on battlefields. None of this negates the fact, however, that these ten American boys deserve to be honored for their willingness to serve their country and fellow man.

At least one of the crew received a Purple Heart, awarded posthumously. In October 1944, Second Lieutenant and Navigator Leonard H. Phillips was awarded the decoration, which was provided to his mother, Libby, because Leonard had "sacrificed his life in defense of his county."[208] Like so many other family members of fallen servicemembers during World War II, Libby never had all her questions about Leonard's death fully answered, but it was not for a lack of asking. On April 10, 1946, Edward F. Witsell, major general, the adjutant general of the army, sent her the names and addresses of the other crew members' next of kin, should she wish to contact them, in the following letter.[209]

> *Dear Mrs. Brown;*
>
> *I am referring to your letter of 10 October 1945, concerning your son, Second Lieutenant Leonard H. Phillips, whose death occurred on 28 June 1943 in the Big Horn Mountains as the result of an airplane crash.*

The distress you have suffered since receiving the sad announcement of your son's death is most understandable and your desire for information regarding him is realized fully. A report has been received in this office which discloses that Lieutenant Phillips was the navigator of a B-17 type aircraft which departed from Pendleton Field, Oregon en route to Grand Island, Nebraska on 28 June 1943 for the purpose of transferring crew and plane to processing unit. The plane was cleared for a formation flight with one other aircraft but for an unknown reason the planes did not fly together but a few minutes. Two widely divergent position reports were received from the aircraft by the control tower at Pendleton Field which were the only known contacts made. When the other plane in the flight landed on schedule at Grand Island search procedures were initiated for the plane on which your son was serving. An aerial search was conducted for seven days over the entire area of the flight but no trace of the plane and its crew was found in spite of favorable weather conditions during this time.

This report further reveals that on 11 August 1945, the Rapid City Army Air Base was notified that the wreckage of a plane had been found near Cloud Peak in the Big Horn Mountains, approximately eighteen miles northeast of Ten Sleep, Wyoming. A search and rescue party was dispatched immediately. The plane was found to have struck about fifty feet below the top edge of a saddleback ridge that rose gradually to the mountain peak, which is an altitude of approximately 13,000 feet. The altitude of the crash was about 12,800 feet. Although the cause of the accident could not be determined due to the complete destruction of the plane and lack of survivors it was thought possible that the plane encountered a thunderstorm and the turbulence threw it down and subsequently into the top of the peak.

The death of your son is deeply regretted and I realize how futile any words of mine may be to assuage your grief but I trust that the knowledge of his heroic sacrifice in action may be a source of sustaining comfort.

Permit me again to extend my sympathy in your bereavement.

Sincerely yours, Edward F. Witsell
Major General

As previously noted, some of the crew members' families and communities memorialized their lives and deaths locally. For Pilot Ronaghan, the New York City Police Department honored his memory by naming a patrol boat after him. A newspaper of the time reported:

In Honor of Her Hero Son
Newest Police Patrol Boat Is Launched; Named for Lost Air Hero, Ex-Patrolman

The Police Department's newest and most modern harbor patrol boat, the Lieutenant Ronaghan, *was launched yesterday at 1:05 P.M., in ceremonies at Randalls Island and, after a brief test run in the East River, joined the department's ten other launches in patrolling and protecting the waters of New York.*

The sixty-foot boat, built at a cost of $30,000, was named after a former patrolman, William R. Ronaghan, who was killed while serving in the Air Force as a B-17 pilot. His mother Mrs. Mary Ronaghan, 1661 Luyting [Lurting] *Avenue, the Bronx, sponsored the boat.*

After a short parade by members of the Army and Navy Union and a brief speech of welcome by Police Commissioner Arthur W. Wallander, Capt. Walter E. Klotzback of the Harbor Precinct placed the boat in commission.

"The orders of the day to the crew of the launch Lieutenant Ronaghan and to all members of the Harbor Precinct," he said, "are to carry on an unrelenting campaign for the protection of life and property on the waters under the jurisdiction of the city of New York, and to be ever mindful of the responsibilities entrusted to your care in maintaining the launch in a condition for instant use."

"Sergeant," he added, "post your platoon."

And Sgt. Frederick W. Mohrmann took command of the vessel and posted his crew of five.

The boat, equipped with two 300 horse-power gasoline engines, demonstrated a speed of 22-miles an hour in its test run. Its equipment includes a two-way radio, flag and light signals, grappling irons, a life saving [sic] *gun and other modern apparatus.*[210]

There has long been an exhibit at the Johnson County Jim Gatchell Memorial Museum in Buffalo, Wyoming, about the crew and the crash. Over the years, the exhibit has undergone many updates and alterations, but the constant theme is that it also acts as a memorial for the crew. The museum staff hopes that the narrative helps visitors understand the region's history and assists them in connecting to the humans who are inextricably woven into that history.

Another group of people made a purposeful and lasting effort to honor the crew as soon as they learned of their demise. At the time the crash site was found in August 1945, there was a nearby local branch of the American War Dads Association, an organization founded to support the parents of active military personnel. Having been started in Kansas City, Kansas, the organization soon had chapters across the United States.[211] Members of the American War Dads Association and Auxiliary, Sheridan Chapter no. 4, acted quickly and secured a large bronze plaque to place near the crash site. A group of about a dozen rode to Florence Lake (which sits directly below the crash site, along the Solitude Trail) and mounted the plaque to a large boulder so that hikers and riders passing by for future generations will know what transpired on those lofty peaks.[212] The year following, the U.S. Forest Service officially christened the mountain as Bomber Mountain after petitioning from various area residents and the Sheridan Chapter no. 4 of the Wyoming State Association of American War Dads.[213] The *Casper-Star Tribune* of Casper and the *News Letter Journal* of Newcastle reported on August 23, 1946, and August 29, respectively, that the U.S. Board of Geographical Names had completed the naming process and at the same

Members of the American War Dads Association and Auxiliary, Sheridan Chapter no. 4, installing the memorial plaque, September 3, 1945. *Schunk family collection.*

time also approved the name Meadowlark Lake for the lake in the Bighorn Mountains that had been created by the Civilian Conservation Corps in 1935 for recreational purposes.

When the American War Dads Association and Auxiliary, Sheridan Chapter no. 4, dedicated the plaque, they also created a memorial document, which narrates their efforts quite eloquently.[214]

In Memorium [sic]

The project of placing a fitting memorial to the memory of the 10 army airmen who lost their lives on June 28, 1943, in the crash of the B-17 Flying Fortress No. 23399 high in the Big Horns was completed last Tuesday with the arrival back in Sheridan of the party late Tuesday evening and Wednesday morning.

Shortly after the news of the disaster was received John D. Van Nest, finance officer, Veterans Administration, Fort Mackenzie, who is president of Sheridan Chapter No. 4, American War Dads, and a veteran of World War I, conceived the idea of erecting a memorial near the spot where the airmen lost their lives in line of duty. He discussed his idea with Dean Johnson of Fort Mackenzie, Dr. William F. Schunk and Howard Sharp, all veterans of World War I, and with others, and received evidence of wholehearted cooperation in the project.

Plans for the difficult trip were laid and the bronze plaque was designed by Van Nest and produced in the plant of the Sheridan Iron Works. The inscription on the plaque reads:

MEMORIAL.

The Following Officers and Enlisted Men of the U.S. Army Air Force Gave Their Lives While on Active Duty in Flight on or About June 28, 1943. Their Bomber Crashed on the Crest of the Mountain Above This Place.

Lieutenants Leonard H. Phillips, Charles H. Suppes, William R. Ronaghan, Anthony J. Tilotta; Sergeants James A. Hinds, Lewis M. Shepard, Charles E. Newburn, Jr., Lee V. Miller, Ferguson T. Bell, Jr., Jake E. Penick.

Dedicated by Sheridan Chapter No. 4, American War Dads and Auxiliary, Sheridan, Wyoming, August, 1945.

Members of the American War Dads Association and Auxiliary, Sheridan Chapter no. 4, at the plaque dedication, September 3, 1945. *Schunk family collection.*

The Wyoming Bomber Crash of 1943

Those who took part in the trip which began Saturday, September 1 were Dr. Schunk, his daughter, Louise; Mr. Van Nest and his son, Fritz; Mr. and Mrs. Joe Driear of the War Dads and auxiliary; Capt. W.E. Landis, M.C., of Fort Warren, Cheyenne; Capt. Willis G. Dick, M.C. of Fort Mackenzie, R.E. Wahl and Dean Johnson, also of Fort Mackenzie; Art Sherwood, secretary-manager of the Sheridan Chamber of Commerce, and Howard Sharp, publisher of The Sheridan Press. *They were joined at the scene of the crash by Ranger I.M. Massey and his son, Bruce.*

The pack outfit left the mountain cabins of Dr. Schunk Sunday morning, September 2, and were joined near Duncan Lake by other members of the party, making a total of 12 persons and 18 horses. They passed Lake Geneva and through Geneva Pass. Then lunch at Crystal Lake and on over Rocky Pass encountering a short shower. Then followed a brief glimpse of the distant Rockies as the sun came out again, arriving at the Lake Solitude camp ground for the night.

The next morning the party began the long trip to the site of the bomber crash. Up, up and up between two forks of the Paint Rock creek, an hour's travel brought a magnificent view of Cloud Peak and the first glimpse of the wrecked plane shimmering in the sunlight. (It is thought that the real reason the plane was not discovered for so long a time, was that the paint blended with the landscape until the elements removed some of it, exposing the bright metal to the sunlight).

Then over Florence Pass at an altitude of 11,900 feet to Florence Lake where the horses were left. Being above timber line, it was necessary to pack in firewood on the horses.

About two hours of difficult climbing up the precipitous mountain side over giant boulders, brought the group to the east side of the ridge where the last remains of the plane came to rest, and where two of the bodies were found by the army officials. At this point was a part of the wings, top gun turret, landing wheels, oxygen tanks, gasoline tanks and wreckage of all description.

Up and over the ridge about one quarter of a mile to the west is where the first impact occured [sic]. *Boulders were shattered and the intense heat of the resulting explosion and fires grumbled the surface of the huge granite boulders. Narrow silver scratches on some of the boulders could be seen, where the propellers first came in contact with the ridge. There is between 100 and 200 feet difference in elevation between where the plane crashed and the summit. Along every foot of the quarter mile distance and far to either side can be seen parts of the ill-fated bomber. The magnitude of the* disaster is almost beyond description and human conception and the group there were awed by the evidence of death and destruction on that fatal 28th of June, 1943.

In the wreckage was found several copies of the order which sent the crew and plane on the last mission, which reads as follows:

"Headquarters, Three Hundred Eighty Third Bombardment Group (H), Geiger Fld. Spokane, Wn. 27 June, 1943. Extract Special orders No. 192. 1. Pursuant to VOCG 2AF of June 17/43, Plumber Prov. Gp, consisting of thirty (30) HBC Crews and supervisory personnel WP by Mil Acft fr Rapid City, S.D., to Pendleton Fld Ore for fur trng under supervision of CO 383rd Bomb Gp (H). At the completion of this trng o/a 28 June 1943, these HBC Crews, accompanied by supervisory personnel WP by Mil Acft to Grand Island, Nebr, RUAT CO 9th HB Proc Unit on or before June 30 for fur asgnt & duty. Auth: 2 AF Memo No. 75-1, Hq 2AF dd Dec. 30/42. A Per Diem of $6.00 per day is auth for both O&EM while participating in aerial flight from Rapid City, S.D. to Pendleton, Ore. & from Pendleton, Ore. to Grand Island, Nebr.

Individual & orgn equipment now on hand or in storage for this Prov. Unit will accompany it in this movement. TDN. 1-5250 P 432-02,03,04,05,-07,08 A 0425-24.

Roster of crews at Plummer Prov. Gp to accompany this order will be furn by CO Plummer Prov Gp when this order is presented for payment purposes. By order of Lt Col Stalder. (Sgd) Henry B. Oestreich, 1st Lt., Air Corps, Adjutant."

This official document is badly weathered and burned slightly. It will be displayed in the Chamber of Commerce office along with numerous other portions of the plane and documents which were recovered by the party.

On the west side of the ridge at the point of impact, and where the wreckage can best be seen from the divide between Lake Solitude and Misty Moon lake was one wing with the plane number "23399" on it, and at the summit was an artist's outfit of paints and colored pencils. It was at this point that the other eight bodies were recovered. Personal effects of all kinds were found, including portions of letters, slightly burned documents, flying caps, shoes, underwear, travel orders, charts and parachutes. Many of these things, and parts of the plane are buried in the crevices of the giant boulders, where they will remain for eternity. One of the landing wheels a quarter of a mile from the point of impact had the huge tire and retracting device still on it. The other wheel nearby was without the tire. The gun turret and a number of the guns were found in the wreckage. A cushion was found which bore the message, "Do not remove from airplane." A partially burned "Mae West" bore the inscription, "Insp. 6/25/43," which was three days before the final journey.

On Solitude Trail

The location of the disaster is described as south and 7 degrees east from Cloud Peak about 1½ miles. The plaque is located on the Solitude Trail near the shore of Florence Lake, 1½ miles south of the bomber remains.

 The army plane, a B-17, destined for a staging base prior to overseas duty, was first discovered by two cowboys, Berl Rader [sic] from the Buck Creek cow camp at Tensleep and Albert Kirkpatrick of Hyattville. Riding the Solitude Trail their curiosity was aroused by a shining object high on the skyline several miles away. Several days later they proceeded to the precipitous slope near Cloud Peak, and discovered the wreckage.

 The two cowboys notified Forest Ranger I.M. Massey at the Tyrrell ranger station and a crew from the search section of the Second air force headquarters at Colorado Springs surveyed the wreckage. On August 13 a party of seven officers and enlisted men from the Rapid City, S.D. air base in charge of Col. William C. Lewis, commanding officer of the base, in company with Herb [Urban] Post, forest ranger in charge of the Hunter ranger station above Buffalo, arrived at the scene of the crash, with a 15-horse pack string. At the same time four army personnel were guided to the spot by Ranger Massey from the West Tensleep entrance.

 The next day the 10 bodies were removed from the wreckage and taken down the mountains as far as the Hunter ranger station where they were transferred to an army ambulance which took them to the Rapid City base.

 On August 18 the identity of the army airmen and the next of kin was announced by the Second army air force headquarters at Colorado Springs, Colo., as follows:

T/Sgt. James A. Hinds, Mrs. Georgia P. Hinds, Manhattan Beach, Calif., wife.
Staff Sgt. Lewis M. Shepard, Mrs. Leo H. Shepard, Jacksonville, Fla., mother.
Second Lt. Charles H. Suppes, Mr. and Mrs. Carl E. Geis, Johnstown, Pa., parents.

Staff Sgt Charles E. Newburn, Jr., Mr. and Mrs. Charles E. Newburn, Wister, Okla., parents.
Second Lt. Leonard H. Phillips, Mrs. Libby M. Brown, Dupont, Colo., mother.
Staff Sgt. Lee V. Miller, Mr. and Mrs. Wilson R. Miller, Glenn Daniel, W.Va., parents.
Staff Sgt. Ferguson T. Bell, Jr., Mrs. Frances D. Bell, Little Rock, Ark., mother.
Second Lt. William R. Ronaghan, Mr. and Mrs. Peter Ronaghan, New York City, parents.
Staff Sgt. Jake F. Penick, Mrs. Dorothy Jo Penick, Cement, Okla., wife.
Second Lt. Anthony J. Tilotta, Mrs. Elsie M. Tilotta, Houston, Tex., wife.

"The American War Dads received eager assistance from many citizens of Sheridan, who felt the place should be marked in honorable fashion. Each citizen participating realized that the long 100-mile pack trip to the scene was arduous both for the people and their horses and pack animals," Mr. Van Nest said.

Copies of this record are to be transmitted to those listed as the nearest of kin so that they may learn that the place where their loved ones made the supreme sacrifice, and were summoned for briefing by the Master Pilot, was not left unmarked or forgotten. The least we can do is to remember and to dedicate ourselves anew to the task of making this world a better place in which to live for those who returned from missions on which they so courageously embarked on our behalf.

The pack train party acknowledges its indebtedness to the following persons who aided so materially in the furtherance of the project by their willing cooperation over and above that which has been anticipated:

H.W. Sterling, Colonel, M.C., manager, Veterans Administration, Sheridan, whose council and official prestige, together with his personal enthusiasm, caused the personnel of his station to carry out the memorial plans.

Dr. Will F. Schunk, Dean Johnson, Jo and Mrs. Driear, whose splendid pack and saddle horses, camp and camp equipment was placed with instant readiness at the service of the expedition, without which the proposed mission might have aborted.

Roy E. Hunnell and Ivan Sprenkel of the Veterans Administration, for the able craftsmanship in the production of the pattern used for casting the tablet; these men worked under considerable handicap turning out a pattern with materials so hard to find.

Mr. P.J. Theisen, manager, Sheridan Iron Works, Sheridan, whose able cooperation and personal interest made it possible to obtain the casting from his foundry in record time so that there would be no undue delay in commencement of travel in view of the possibility of severe storms in the high mountains at this season of the year.

Bighorn National Forest whose supervisor, Mr. William B. Fay, gave us the benefit of his wisdom and experience adding much to insure success of the project. Also Ranger Massey, whose knowledge of the wilderness area of the Big Horns and trails, further insured against miscarriage of our plans.

Officers and members of Sheridan Chapter 4, American War Dads and Auxiliary, who approved the proposal and made the project possible.

Mr. Bert Brooks, proprietor, Big Horn Monument company, Sheridan, whose loan of stone dressing tools and equipment and expert instruction insured the proper and permanent affixing of the plaque to the stone.

Kibben Hardware company, Sheridan, whose courtesy in extending use of the main display window enabling hundreds of citizens to view the memorial before it started on its journey.

And to many others who instantly rendered advice, aid and active assistance which in this busy world means so much when undertakings of this nature are attempted.

As this wrecked airship brought the hazards of war very close to Sheridan, and is the only incident of its kind of record in this vicinity it is hoped by the sponsoring group that in addition to the placement of the memorial on the Solitude Trail, the forest service will give the peak which caused the catastrophe an appropriate name, such as "Bomber Peak" and also name the unnamed lake below Florence lake in memory of the tragedy.[215]

After the party returned from the mountain top a site was selected for the plaque and dedication ceremony took place with Dean Johnson calling for *remarks from Ranger Massey, Mr. Sharp, Mr. Van Nest, Mrs. Driear and Mr. Sherwood. A prayer given by Captain Dick and a salute fired by Dr. Schunk concluded the ceremony, as tears stood in the eyes of every member of the party.*

Thus sojourners and travelers who pass along the trail, viewing the incomparable scenery on every hand, will come up on the tablet and be reminded of what so many owe to these men. They will be reminded also, of the fact that the gigantic mountain stands as an eternal monument over the scene of their death; another shrine marking the spot where brave Americans fell in the service of the country and to those who flew the great bombers on missions from which so many never returned.

And so at 4:45 p.m. on Monday, Sept. 3, 1945, on a lonely granite boulder on the Solitude Trail, high in the Cloud Peak wilderness was placed the memorial to the 10 members of the army air forces, who gave their lives in line of duty. The group, representing the entire Sheridan community, paid its final tribute to their memory. (Reprinted with permission of Sheridan Press.*)*

A close-up view of the plaque in 2009. *Author's collection.*

The Wyoming Bomber Crash of 1943

The Wyoming Bomber Crash of 1943

Louise Schunk in front of a portion of the wreckage, September 3, 1945. *Schunk family collection.*

Copies of records in the Bighorn National Forest Historical Collection housed at the Jim Gatchell Memorial Museum offer further information about the plaque and the efforts to memorialize the crew. A letter from I.M. (Irving) Massey, forest ranger, Tensleep, Wyoming, to the forest supervisor in Sheridan, dated December 10, 1945, is an answer to a letter that apparently requested information about the location of the plaque. Massey described the plaque as being on the east side of the Solitude Trail, near the Florence Lake outlet. He also noted that the plaque was located on the Buffalo District (now known as the Powder River Ranger District), and he was sending information to Ranger Post (Urban Post) in case Post had any additional information to include for the supervisor (William Fay).[216] Massey and Post were both present at the recovery in August 1945, and Massey was also present at the plaque dedication that September, so he would have been very familiar with its location.

Another letter in this collection, addressed to William Fay, Bighorn National Forest supervisor, was from John D. Van Nest, representing the Wyoming State Association of American War Dads. His letter was also in response to a query from Fay, in which he had apparently asked the War Dads if they supported naming the site "Bomber Mountain," to which Van Nest wrote that they "concur heartily in the name." This correspondence was from February 1946, which again demonstrates the gravity and speed with which the region's residents paid their respects to the crew.[217]

While residents in Wyoming worked to honor the crew, their families were picking up the pieces and moving forward with their lives. Wives remarried, and children grew up, but the unanswered questions about what had happened to the crew never left the minds of their loved ones. Billy Ronaghan's sister Florence had married Thomas Veale in 1949 and was building her own life and family but continued to wonder about what happened to Billy. In the 1950s, she reached out to newspapers in the region around the crash site. In February 1956, she received an answering letter from Helen Turner of Hyattville, Wyoming, a small town on the western side of the Bighorn Mountains. Turner wrote:

Hyattville, Wyoming, February 7, 1956
Dear Mrs. Veale:

As you know, your letter to the publisher of the Northern Wyoming Daily news has been referred to me because I was the editor of the paper at the time of the plane crash you ask about, and my husband was among the first on the scene.

The Wyoming Bomber Crash of 1943

Perhaps it would be best if I began at the beginning and told the story as I knew it at the time. I had not lived in Hyattville very long at the time, because my husband and I had just been married a short time before and I was still helping out at the newspaper office whenever called upon.

Jack and I were at a bridge party in August of 1945, when I overheard some men in the kitchen talking about a plane crash. I had been a reporter too long not to start inquirring [sic] *at once. The two men who had found the plane were Berl Bader, whose address is Hyattville, and Albert Kirkpatrick, whose address is Basin, Wyoming. I didn't know the men at the time and do not recall which one I talked to. I think it was Albert* [Berl was typed first, but then it was scratched out]. *The story as told at the time was like this:*

The two men were cowboys (not mountain climbers) and were on a roundup on the mountains. I believe a large crew was doing some branding etc. Anyway, on one occasion as they were riding directly toward the mountain peak (which has since been named Bomber Mountain), a brilliant light hit them in the eyes. They felt positive that it must be a reflection from some very bright metal. The men talked about it and some of them ridiculed the idea, of course, but after the work was done and the other men had returned home, Berl and Albert decided to ride up there and satisfy their curiosity. It is no easy trip and I believe the last ascent had to be made on foot. The peak is one of the highest in the Big Horn range and is rocky and barren at the top. It is right next to Cloud Peak which is 13,165 feet high, the very highest in the range. The month of August is the only month during which the snow is gone from the peak, so doubtless at no other time could the wreckage have been seen, and that accounts for the fact that it was over two years before it was found. Well, anyway, the men climbed up, discovered the wrecked B-17, and left quite soon. They did report, however, to the ranger, I believe, as soon as possible. Now perhaps these men could tell you more, but neither is apt to write much, because it is just out of their line to do so. I saw Berl in the post office a few days ago, but he was very reluctant to talk. So I'll leave that part of the story and go on to my husband's account.

The next day after we heard about it, my husband and a friend by the name of A.E. Greer and his stepson, Jack Skeen, took horses in a jeep, drove as far as they could, rode as far as they could, and finally climbed to the scene. Jack says that on the way up the trail, they met a party of dudes from Sheridan coming out. They had a few things they had picked up for souvenirs, mostly parts of the plane, I think.

I hate to destroy your mother's hope that her son may be alive, but anyone who could see the wreckage would know that such a thing would be utterly impossible. Even had a person survived, he could never have made it out of there at that time of the year, for the snow would have been deep in June and the peak is at least thirty miles or more from any habitation.

Jack says the plane lacked only a few feet of clearing the peak and looked as though the front had gotten over and the tail had hit, completely wrecking the plane. Parts are scattered over a wide area. The metal hit the rocks and was curled into odd shapes and melted from the heat. The bodies were not burned, however, but due to the coldness of the weather, were in some cases well preserved. Jack said the pilot had been thrown against a rock and was sort of hanging over it and could have been recognized by anyone who had known him. Parts of other bodies were scattered for many feet, but they could tell that there were ten persons aboard. So big are the rocks that there are crevices many feet deep and impossible to reach, of course. Parts of the plane were down in these crevices and remain there to this day. Shoes were curled up as leather does when exposed to the weather and they saw wallets much the same, but one of the big mysteries is that no one found a cent of money on the scene. As Jack and his party left, they met the army men going in to bring out the bodies.

We always expected the FBI to make investigation as to what happened to the money, which was certain to have been in some of the wallets. There is the belief around Hyattville that an old hermit by the name of Jake Johnson came upon the wreckage some time before and never reported it. He was half-crazy and roamed the mountains staking claims. He was known to have had a wad of bills some time afterward, but the authorities never checked on him, and he has since died. I, personally, feel sure he had found it, taken what he wanted, and kept still about the whole thing. He was just the type to do such a thing.

As I said at first, I was editor of the paper at the time, and I asked the sheriff at Worland for a follow-up on the story, but he refused to give me anything else and told me not to run any more on it, for security reasons. So, from that point on, I know nothing about it except that it has been visited by quite a few persons around here. A woman by the name of Mrs. Raymond Gossens, address Ten Sleep, Wyoming, has some slides which she showed recently of the plane as she saw it on a trip there last summer or the summer before. They are in color and show the mountain scene well. If you would care to have such a picture, I feel sure she is the kind of person who would be glad to send you one if you wrote her for it.

As we heard here, the plane had refueled at Casper, Wyoming, which is in the central part of Wyoming. To go to Grand Island takes them over perfectly *level country. How or why they were off their route, no one will ever know, but of course they would not be expecting mountain peaks such as those in this area. The country around Casper is about 4,000 feet I expect.*

It does seem that the government could have found something of a personal nature to send each family, yet it is conceivable that such a thing was impossible, considering the way everything was scattered. I suppose there are innumerable things there yet, such as the identification tag you received, which will be found from time to time.

I don't know what else I can tell you. If you have questions, I would be most happy to answer them for you. I know how painful all this must be to you, but I know that you wanted to know the truth. I could add that your brother couldn't have suffered, because death would have come instantly and very likely while many of them were asleep. It would almost certainly have been at night or the tragedy would not have happened at all. If you should ever come to Wyoming, do make it a point to come to our ranch. If there were anything we could do for you, we would be most happy to do it.

Sincerely yours, Helen Turner

A few things about this letter need to be addressed. While Turner was most certainly trying to be helpful to the Ronaghan family, she included several misconceptions and substantial misinformation. From her letter, it is apparent that she had not visited the crash site in person but was relaying secondhand stories years after the fact. Breaking down the information available, we know that the other members of the cattle association had not gone home, and in fact, many or most of them had also climbed to the crash site. Although August is generally a good month to access the site, it is certainly not a hard and fast rule that you cannot get there before or after. The site is only about twenty-three miles west of Buffalo. The bodies were most definitely burned. This fact is verified in the military crash report, in the accident investigator's personal diary and in the records from the South Dakota funeral home that processed the remains before they were sent to their respective homes for burial. It is very likely and understandable that Jack Turner did not know the difference between a burned body and one that had suffered from exposure.

The Federal Bureau of Investigation would not have been called in to investigate the crash, as there was no indication that a crime had occurred.[218] Regarding her accusation that Jake Johnson stole any cash present—well, it is doubtful that there was much to start with, as these men were being deployed, and most, if not all of them were in the habit of sending a substantial portion of their pay home to their families. There is no known record of this aircraft carrying any kind of payroll or money. It is also useful to remember that Ronaghan's wallet was identified and retrieved by the military investigators, and evidence of cash was still present. It seems particularly unnecessary to lob an accusation of theft toward a deceased man who could not defend himself.

There is no evidence or documentation that the plane refueled in Casper, and lastly, the military absolutely did attempt to return the crew members' effects they found at the site and which they could match to a particular crew member. For instance, there were photographs and small items on Leonard Phillips's body (only his torso was found and identified) that were returned to his mother.[219] It is sobering to realize the task of finding and returning items may have been easier for military investigators to accomplish had local residents not immediately visited the site and retrieved "souvenirs" before the bodies were even recovered.

A gentle reminder for those intending to visit the site: please not remove or alter it in any way—do not take pieces of the wreckage and do not leave memorabilia of your own. Instead, think of these bright young men whose futures were laid out in front of them until a fateful night in 1943. Then maybe give them and our nation's other honorable veterans just a tip of your hat in respect.

AFTERWORD

Research into this event has distinct limitations, as it was not a long chapter in history with multiple perspectives to explore. Primary sources regarding the crash are slim, and there is only so much that can be said about an accident, even if it was a horrific one. However, the people involved are always at the heart of any historical tale. Given the young age of the crew, most had not accumulated a large number of accomplishments or public accolades for a researcher to find years later, and their military records are sparse at best. The 1973 fire at the National Personnel Records Center destroyed a lot of American history, as much of the nation's veterans' records were (and still are) housed there.[220] Some files were only partially burned, and others have been reconstructed by gathering information held at other sites. However, individual deceased personnel files (IDPF) were available for most of the ten crewmen, and although limited, they contained records that provided useful information, such as casualty reports, applications for grave markers and documents generated by the funeral home in South Dakota that processed the remains. It is worth pointing out that a few of the men's files also contained copies of their dental records. Many of the crew members' bodies were decapitated and so badly mangled during the crash that it is plausible these records were needed in 1945 to verify the identification of the remains recovered from the site.

Though it was one of the biggest conflicts in the history of the world, World War II was full of coincidences and connections. My paternal grandfather was working as a riveter at Douglas's Long Beach, California aircraft plant during the time it produced block 55, which included the *Scharazad*. There is a possibility that my ancestor worked on this particular aircraft during production, but that is another question that will never be directly answered, as he is long gone from this world, and it is doubtful that records exist that could verify or disprove this possibility. Another coincidence noted during research is that when Leonard Phillips completed his aerial navigation training at Hondo Army Air Field, Texas, he graduated with a slew of other men, one of them being a Daniel John Maher, whose address was 1660 Lurting Avenue, Bronx, New York, literally the house across the street from Pilot William R. Ronaghan's family home, which was located at 1661 Lurting Avenue.[221]

In 1984, the crash site was encompassed by the newly formed Cloud Peak Wilderness, but the location has always been remote and difficult to get to, as it requires a scramble up the mountainside to an elevation of around twelve thousand feet after a hike or horseback ride of at least seven miles. This does not deter many from visiting the crash site, however, and the area is heavily trafficked by backpackers. A 2016 compilation of Cloud Peak Wilderness user data by the Bighorn National Forest offices in Buffalo recorded that over 34,500 people registered to use the West Tensleep Trailhead, one of the most popular routes to the site. Of that number, over 13,000 listed their destination as Bomber Mountain.[222] As the U.S. Air Force determined none of the wreckage was worth retrieving in 1945, the thousands of pieces of the wreckage were left in place at that time. Fast-forwarding to current times, a shocking amount of the aircraft is missing due to people scavenging pieces while visiting the site. Many who visit may not know that in 1966, the site fell under protection of the National Historic Preservation Act, and in 1979, it was also protected by the Archaeological Resources Protection Act, both of which prevent further desecration of a site that many view as hallowed ground.[223]

As this history has long been of interest to me, one obvious place to visit was the crash site itself. The site requires no technical knowledge or experience to access, as it is not a rock-climbing event. But reaching it does require a person to be in good health, as it is a strenuous scramble up the mountain over rocks large and small, and you cannot ride a horse, mule or vehicle to the site. Some people, like this author, also experience altitude sickness, which can be physically debilitating and incredibly frustrating when you are trying to absorb the surroundings but your body is recoiling from the lack of oxygen and insisting you descend to normalcy.

Afterword

Rubber adhered to a rock on the west side of Bomber Mountain, August 9, 2014. *Author's collection.*

Pieces of metal plating in the debris field, August 9, 2014. *Author's collection.*

Afterword

A small portion of the debris field, August 9, 2014. *Author's collection.*

View of debris field, August 9, 2014. *Author's collection.*

Afterword

Looking down toward Mistymoon Lake from Bomber Mountain, August 9, 2014. *Author's collection.*

Further debris on the east side of Bomber Mountain, August 9, 2014. *Author's collection.*

Afterword

Nevertheless, in August 2014, my husband and I made the trip to Mistymoon Lake on horseback/muleback from Battle Park. All of Bomber Mountain and the surrounding area is contained within the Cloud Peak Wilderness, and there are no motorized or wheeled vehicles allowed, so the campground at Battle Park was as close as we could get with our truck and horse trailer. The ride in featured a fierce hailstorm, followed by rain, and wrapped up with a second hailstorm.

Having allowed ourselves a three-day weekend to accomplish this visit, we camped overnight just beyond Mistymoon Lake and had a full day to climb to the crash site and explore. We ascended the ridge from the west and then walked the to the north until we came across the first pieces of debris—mainly, the vertical stabilizer (or tail). From there, we hop-scotched from piece to piece, trying to figure out what each item used to be. It became easier to disassociate from the gravity of the place as we found mostly metal pieces, cables and wood bits. But then finding something like the remains of a deep yellow life vest (humorously called a Mae West vest by soldiers at the time) would jolt us back into thinking of the humans who were involved.[224]

Part of one of the engine turbochargers, August 9, 2014. *Author's collection.*

136

Afterword

We carefully folded the vest and tucked it among the boulders. As we moved from piece to piece, it seemed the debris field was ever-increasing in size. Just when we thought we were at the outer edges, we would spy another bit of metal farther away. Much of the plane is located directly above Florence Lake, and from that vantage point, a person has an amazing view down Florence Pass along the Solitude Trail.

The number of missing pieces of the plane was shocking to us. Steering yokes, oxygen tanks, machine guns, ten of the twelve propeller blades—all missing. It felt as though any identifiable part that could humanly be packed out had been taken. Much of what remains on the mountain has been covered in graffiti by visiting hikers. Pieces of the front landing gear wheel's rubber has been cut out, and names have been carved on the two remaining propeller blades and aluminum skin.

The sheer destruction of the aircraft was also shocking. My husband stated that it was as though the plane "had gone through a cheese grater," and that is the most succinct description I have heard yet. It no longer a plane; it is a debris field. As excited as I was to be at the site, knowing that ten very

Looking down on Florence Lake and Florence Pass, where the memorial plaque resides, August 9, 2014. *Author's collection.*

Afterword

Larger pieces of debris on the east side of Bomber Mountain, August 9, 2014. *Author's collection.*

Image of the tail stabilizer taken on August 14, 1945. *United States Army Air Corps.*

Afterword

Image of the propeller blades taken on August 14, 1945. *United States Army Air Corps.*

Image of the propeller blades taken on August 9, 2014. *Author's collection.*

Image of the Sperry top turret with an ammunition box and components still present, August 14, 1945. *United States Army Air Corps.*

young men lost their lives there tempered my joy with the somberness that comes with respect for those lost. The oldest crew member was James Alfred Hinds at twenty-five. Twenty-five. That's it. These men had only scratched the surface of their lives' potentials. All these young men should have had many years ahead of them, and I cannot help but wonder: Who would they have become?

NOTES

Chapter 1

1. Westmont Presbyterian Church, dedication.
2. Bowers, *50th Anniversary*, 65.
3. 447th Bomb Group, "*Scheherazade.*"
4. *Encyclopædia Britannica*, "*The Thousand and One Nights.*"
5. *The Phoenician*, Westmont-Upper Yoder High School.
6. PBS, "Air War."
7. *Encyclopædia Britannica*, "Marshaling Yard"; Linn, "Boeing B-17."
8. Museum of Flight, "Boeing B-17F Flying Fortress."
9. *Army Air Forces Statistical Digest*, 15.
10. *Army Air Forces Statistical Digest*, 14, 184.
11. *Army Air Forces Statistical Digest*, 310.
12. Freeman, *Flying Fortress Story*, 31–32.
13. Hangar Thirteen, "Aircraft Camouflage."
14. Yenne, *Building the B-17*, 92.
15. Aero Vintage Books, "B-17 Production List."
16. Joseph F. Baugher, "1942 USAAF Serial Numbers"; Joseph Baugher, email to the author, September 3, 2015; Smithsonian National Air and Space Museum, "Aircraft Record Card."
17. Yenne, *Building the B-17*, 122, 126, 136.
18. Jablonski, *Flying Fortress*, 34.
19. Yenne, *Building the B-17*, 7.
20. Smithsonian National Air and Space Museum, "Aircraft Record Card."

21. Smithsonian National Air and Space Museum, "Aircraft Record Card."
22. Shepard, letter to Leo Hazel Shepard, June 17, 1943.
23. Maurer, *Combat Squadrons*, 388, 646, 647; Maurer, *Air Force Combat Units*, 154, 270.
24. United States Army Air Corps, "Leonard Harvey Phillips."
25. Horwitz, letter to Ronaghan.

Chapter 2

26. Veale, email to the author, May 20, 2024.
27. Veale, "Babe," 5–7.
28. Veale, email to the author, April 30, 2024.
29. Unidentified newspaper, "Airman Is Reported Missing."
30. *The Oriole*, Evander Childs High School.
31. "Enlistment Record," Ronaghan Family Collection, Jim Gatchell Memorial Museum.
32. Ronaghan Veale, interview with the author.
33. O'Brien, letter to commanding general.
34. Mentzinger, letter of reference.
35. Conway, letter to Ronaghan.
36. "George Field Army Flying School," Ronaghan Family Collection, Jim Gatchell Memorial Museum.
37. Veale, "Babe," 5–7.
38. Department of the Army, "William Ronaghan"; "Enlistment Record," Ronaghan Family Collection, Jim Gatchell Memorial Museum.
39. "Duties and Responsibilities," in *B-17 Pilot Training Manual*, 13–14.
40. Ronaghan Veale, interview with the author.
41. Unidentified newspaper, "Mass Is Said."
42. Valentine, letter to Ronaghan.
43. Unidentified newspaper, "Bluecoats Launch a Memorial."
44. Armed Forces Memorial Wall Ceremony.
45. Ronaghan Veale, interview with the author.

Chapter 3

46. Find a Grave, "Anthony Joseph Tilotta."
47. Davis, email with the author, March 19, 2024.
48. U.S. Census Bureau, 1930 census, Harris County, TX.
49. Davis, email with the author, March 19, 2024.
50. United States Naturalization Service, "Petition for Naturalization."
51. Davis, email with the author, March 19, 2024.
52. Davis, email with the author, March 19, 2024.

53. Davis, email with the author, March 19, 2024.
54. Marriage license, Harris County, TX, July 17, 1941; Davis, personal correspondence.
55. Davis, email with the author, March 19, 2024.
56. Tilotta Family Collection, "Blackland Army Flying School."
57. "Duties and Responsibilities," in *B-17 Pilot Training Manual*, 14–15.
58. Department of the Army, "Anthony Joseph Tilotta."
59. Marriage license, Harris County, TX, August 3, 1948; Davis, email with the author, January 7, 2020.

Chapter 4

60. United States Army Air Corps, "Leonard Harvey Phillips."
61. Marriage license, Big Horn County, MT, May 2, 1926.
62. Marriage license, Big Horn County, MT, May 2, 1926.
63. "Fisher Rites," *Wyoming State Tribune*.
64. United States Army Air Corps, "Leonard Harvey Phillips."
65. United States Army Air Corps, "Leonard Harvey Phillips."
66. John & Ann Gallentine.
67. Brooks and Brooks, personal interview.
68. United States Army Air Corps, "Leonard Harvey Phillips," (Personal History Statement).
69. United States Army Air Corps, "Leonard Harvey Phillips."
70. Brooks and Brooks, personal interview.
71. United States Army Air Corps, "Leonard Harvey Phillips," (Application for Appointment as Aviation Cadet).
72. United States Army Air Corps, "Leonard Harvey Phillips," (Personal History Statement).
73. United States Army Air Corps, "Leonard Harvey Phillips," (Personal Placement Questionnaire).
74. United States Army Air Corps, "Leonard Harvey Phillips."
75. United States Army Air Corps, "Leonard Harvey Phillips."
76. United States Army Air Corps, "Leonard Harvey Phillips."
77. United States Army Air Corps, "Leonard Harvey Phillips," (Application for Appointment as Aviation Cadet).
78. United States Army Air Corps, "Leonard Harvey Phillips."
79. United States Army Air Corps, "Leonard Harvey Phillips."
80. United States Army Air Corps, "Leonard Harvey Phillips."
81. United States Army Air Corps, "Leonard Harvey Phillips."
82. United States Army Air Corps, "Leonard Harvey Phillips."
83. "Duties and Responsibilities," in *B-17 Pilot Training Manual*, 15–18.

84. United States Army Air Corps, "Leonard Harvey Phillips."
85. United States Army Air Corps, "Leonard Harvey Phillips."
86. United States Army Air Corps, "Leonard Harvey Phillips," (Army Air Forces Navigation School, Hondo Army Air Field, Texas, April 21, 1943).
87. United States Army Air Corps, "Leonard Harvey Phillips."
88. United States Army Air Corps, "Leonard Harvey Phillips."
89. United States Army Air Corps, "Leonard Harvey Phillips."

Chapter 5

90. Westmont Presbyterian Church, dedication; Suppes, personal correspondence with the author.
91. World War II Veterans' Compensation Bureau, "Application for World War II Compensation."
92. *The Phoenician*, Westmont-Upper Yoder High School; *Encyclopædia Britannica*, "Hi-Y Clubs."
93. *The Phoenician*, Westmont-Upper Yoder High School.
94. Westmont Presbyterian Church, dedication.
95. Suppes, personal correspondence with the author.
96. "Duties and Responsibilities," in *B-17 Pilot Training Manual*, 18–22.
97. Maguire, *Silver Wings, Pinks & Greens*, 95.
98. Air Force's Personnel Center, "Army Good Conduct Medal."
99. Air Force's Personnel Center, "American Defense Service Medal."
100. National Air and Space Museum, "American Campaign Medal."
101. World War II Veterans' Compensation Bureau, "Application for World War II Compensation."

Chapter 6

102. "Hinds," World War II Draft Registration Cards for California.
103. *Boomer*, El Reno High School, 1938.
104. "Cridermen Await Invasion," *El Reno Daily Tribune*.
105. El Reno Athletics, "We Remember."
106. Hinds, personal interview.
107. Hinds, personal interview; United States Army Air Corps, "Leonard Harvey Phillips."
108. Hinds, email to the author, March 31, 2024.
109. Wolfenbarger, letter to Bader.
110. "Hinds Found by Cowboys," *Manhattan Beach News*.
111. "Hinds Found by Cowboys," *Manhattan Beach News*.
112. "Duties and Responsibilities," in *B-17 Pilot Training Manual*, 24.

113. "Hinds in Yuma Wedding," *Redondo Reflex*.
114. Gary McAulay (Manhattan Beach Historical Society), email correspondence with the author, 2014–18; Gary McAulay, email to the author, April 3, 2024.

Chapter 7

115. U.S. Census Bureau, 1910 census, Delaware County, PA.
116. "Thomasville Flyer," *Selma Times-Journal*; "Selective Service Registration: Ferguson Theodore Bell Jr."
117. U.S. Census Bureau, 1900 census, Delaware County, PA.
118. *Yearbook*, Williamson Free School of Mechanical Trades.
119. U.S. Census Bureau, 1920 census, Shoshoni, WY; U.S. Census Bureau, 1920 census, Riverton, WY.
120. Marriage license, Hot Springs, WY.
121. Charleston City Directory.
122. U.S. Census Bureau, 1930 census, Monticello Village, NY.
123. U.S. Census Bureau, 1940 census, Thomasville, AL.
124. Florida Divorce Index, Lee, FL.
125. "Thomasville Flyer," *Selma Times-Journal*.
126. U.S. Census Bureau, 1940 census, Thomasville, AL.
127. "Dunning Passes," *Selma Times-Journal*; Wiberg, "Sail and Steam Cargo Vessels from Bahamas"; American Merchant Marine at War, "Merchant Mariners Killed"; "Alabamians on Casualty List," *Birmingham News*.
128. Department of the Army, "Ferguson Theodore Bell."
129. Department of the Army, "Ferguson Theodore Bell."
130. "Duties and Responsibilities," in *B-17 Pilot Training Manual*, 23.
131. "Wreckage Found in Big Horns," *The Sheridan Press*; U.S. Census Bureau, 1950 census, Baraboo, WI.
132. U.S. Department of Defense, "Victory Over Japan Day."
133. Department of the Army, "Ferguson Theodore Bell."
134. Department of the Army, "Ferguson Theodore Bell."

Chapter 8

135. Bair, telephone interview.
136. Miller, letter to Wilson Miller, August 6, 1942.
137. "Wilson R. Miller," *The Advocate-Messenger*.
138. Bair, telephone interview.
139. "Twenty-Seven Candidates," *Raleigh Register*.
140. Moore, "Dickens Biography"; Cooper, "Little Jimmy Dickens."
141. National Archives and Records Administration, "Lee Vaughan Miller."

142. Miller, letter to Wilson Miller, July 7, 1942.
143. Miller, letter to Wilson Miller, August 6, 1942.
144. *Beckley Post-Herald*, December 4, 1942; Miller, letter to Wilson Miller, August 6, 1942; "Body of Glen Daniel Soldier Found," *Raleigh Register*.
145. *Wendover Aerial Gunnery School* (photograph).
146. "Duties and Responsibilities," in *B-17 Pilot Training Manual*, 24–25.
147. Bair and Bair, personal interview.
148. "Body of Glen Daniel Soldier Found," *Raleigh Register*.

Chapter 9

149. "Selective Service Registration: Charles Edgar Newburn."
150. Find a Grave, "Helen Myers Newburn."
151. Newburn, personal interview with author.
152. "Duties and Responsibilities," in *B-17 Pilot Training Manual*, 23, 25.
153. "Wister Boy Sent Home," unidentified newspaper.
154. The Historical Marker Database, "Sioux Falls Army Technical School."
155. U.S. Army Corps of Engineers, "Fort Myers."
156. Desert Training Center, "Blyth Army Airfield."
157. Newburn, personal interview with author.

Chapter 10

158. National Archives and Records Administration, "Jake Floyd Penick."
159. Goolsby, "Winds of Change."
160. National Archives and Records Administration, "Jake Floyd Penick."
161. U.S. Census Bureau, 1940 census, Houston County, TX.
162. National Archives and Records Administration, "Jake Floyd Penick."
163. National Archives and Records Administration, "Jake Floyd Penick."
164. Living New Deal, "Davy Crockett National Forest"; Forest Service, "Davy Crockett National Forest."
165. National Archives and Records Administration, "Jake Floyd Penick."
166. Department of the Army, "Jake Floyd Penick."
167. Debra Penick McDonald, email to the author, February 9, 2015.
168. Find a Grave, "Iva L. Floyd Penick."
169. Marriage Record no. 30, Comanche County, OK, August 2, 1941.
170. "Duties and Responsibilities," in *B-17 Pilot Training Manual*, 25.
171. "Body of Sgt. Jake Penick Found," unidentified newspaper.

Chapter 11

172. Jack Shepard and Pamela Shepard, email to the author, January 28, 2015.
173. U.S. Census Bureau, 1940 census, Jacksonville, FL.
174. Jack Shepard, interview with the author.
175. Department of the Army, "Lewis Marvin Shepard" (August 20, 1948, U.S. Army Human Resources Command).
176. "Crash Victim's Rites," unidentified newspaper.
177. Pamela Shepard, telephone interview with the author.
178. United States Army Air Forces Technical School diploma.
179. Shepard, letter to Leo Hazel Shepard, n.d.
180. "Duties and Responsibilities," in *B-17 Pilot Training Manual*, 25.
181. Western Union Telegrams, August 18 and August 19, 1945.
182. Department of the Army, "Lewis Marvin Shepard."

Chapter 12

183. United States Army Air Forces, "Description of Accident"; an approximately 1,080-mile flight with a six-hour flight duration was divided roughly in half, as the crash site is about 570 miles from Pendleton Field.
184. United States Army Air Corps, "Leonard Harvey Phillips."
185. United States Army Air Forces, "Description of Accident."
186. Edwards, *Aerial View*.
187. United States Army Air Corps, "Leonard Harvey Phillips."

Chapter 13

188. United States Army Air Forces, "Description of Accident."
189. United States Army Air Forces, "Description of Accident."
190. Shepard, letter to Leo Hazel Shepard, n.d.
191. Hamm, personal diary, August 9–August 30, 1945.
192. "Wreckage, Bodies," *The Montana Standard*.

Chapter 14

193. "Flyers Identified Who Died," *Seminole Producer*; "10 Bodies Removed," *Miami News*; "Bodies Found," *Missoulian*.
194. "Wreckage of Plane Found," *Casper Star-Tribune*.
195. "Bodies, Plane Found," *Lexington Herald*.
196. "Bodies Recovered," *Wichita Falls Times*.
197. "Thomasville Flyer," *The Clarke County Democrat*.

198. "Identify 6," *Evening Courier*.
199. "Army Identifies Bodies," *Billings Gazette*.
200. United States Army Air Forces, "Description of Accident."; Hamm, personal diary, August 9–August 30, 1945.
201. "Forestry and Air Force Men Start," *Casper Star-Tribune*.
202. Hamm, personal diary, August 9–August 30, 1945.
203. United States Army Air Forces, "Description of Accident."
204. Department of the Army, "Lewis Marvin Shepard."
205. Department of the Army, "Lewis Marvin Shepard."

Chapter 15

206. "Hamm Dies," *Rock Springs Daily Rocket-Miner*; Hamm, personal diary, August 9–August 30, 1945.
207. "Hamm Dies," *Rock Springs Daily Rocket-Miner*.

Chapter 17

208. United States Army Air Corps, "Leonard Harvey Phillips."
209. United States Army Air Corps, "Leonard Harvey Phillips."
210. "Patrol Boat Is Launched," unidentified newspaper.
211. *Encyclopedia Dubuque*, "American War Dads."
212. American War Dads and Auxiliary, memorial.
213. Van Nest, letter to Fay.
214. American War Dads and Auxiliary, memorial.
215. Fortress or Gunboat Lake.
216. Massey, letter to forest supervisor.
217. Massey, letter to forest supervisor.
218. FBI, "What We Investigate."
219. United States Army Air Corps, "Leonard Harvey Phillips."

Afterword

220. Stender and Walker, "National Personnel Records Center Fire," 521–49.
221. United States Army Air Corps, "Official Military Personnel File: Leonard Harvey Phillips. Special Orders No. 95."
222. Grubb, electronic correspondence.
223. National Historic Preservation Act; GovInfo, "Archaeological Resources Protection Act."
224. Army Air Corps Library and Museum, "Survival Vests."

BIBLIOGRAPHY

The Advocate-Messenger. "Wilson R. Miller." December 5, 1975.
Aero Vintage Books. "B-17 Production List." January 27, 2022. https://www.aerovintage.com/b-17-production-list/.
Air Force's Personnel Center. "American Defense Service Medal." https://www.afpc.af.mil/Fact-Sheets/Display/Article/421948/american-defense-service-medal/.
———. "Army Good Conduct Medal." https://www.afpc.af.mil/Fact-Sheets/Display/Article/421873/army-good-conduct-medal/.
American Merchant Marine at War. "American Merchant Mariners Killed in World War II, Names Start with 'D.'" http://www.usmm.org/killed/d.html.
American War Dads and Auxiliary, Sheridan Chapter no. 4, 1945. Memorial. Sheridan, WY. Bighorn National Forest Historical Collection, Jim Gatchell Memorial Museum.
Armed Forces Memorial Wall Ceremony. Ronaghan Family Collection, Jim Gatchell Memorial Museum. May 30, 2007.
Army Air Corps Museum. "Mae West Survival Vests." https://www.armyaircorpsmuseum.org/Mae_Wests.cfm.
Army Air Forces Statistical Digest: World War II. Office of Statistical Control, 1945.
Bair, Nancy. Telephone interview with the author. April 9, 2024.
Bair, Nancy, and John Bair. Personal interview with the author. July 4, 2013.
Beckley Post-Herald. December 4, 1942.
Billings Gazette. "Army Identifies Bodies of Men." August 19, 1945.
Birmingham News. "54 Alabamians on Casualty List of Freight Ships." September 29, 1942.
Boomer. El Reno High School, 1938.
Bowers, Peter M. *50th Anniversary Boeing B-17 Flying Fortress: 1935–1985*. Museum of Flight, 1985.

Bibliography

Brooks, Wheldon, and Merrice Brooks (Leonard Harvey Phillips's classmates). Telephone interview with the author. January 26, 2016.

Casper Star-Tribune. "Forestry and Air Force Men Start for Wreckage." August 14, 1945.

———. "Wreckage of Plane Found on Cloud Peak, Six Dead." August 13, 1945.

Charleston City Directory. Charleston, SC. 1925.

The Clarke County Democrat. "Thomasville Flyer Is Plane Crash Victim." August 23, 1945.

Conway, Clark. Letter to William Ronaghan. October 30, 1939. Ronaghan Family Collection, Jim Gatchell Memorial Museum.

Cooper, Peter. "Little Jimmy Dickens, Beloved *Opry* Star, Dies at 94." *Tennessean*, January 6, 2015. https://www.tennessean.com/story/entertainment/2015/01/02/little-jimmy-dickens-opry-star-dies-obit/21210809/.

Davis, Mike. Email with the author. January 7, 2020.

———. Email with the author. March 19, 2024.

Department of the Army. "Individual Deceased Personnel File: Anthony Joseph Tilotta." U.S. Army Human Resources Command. N.d.

———. "Individual Deceased Personnel File: Charles Edgar Newburn." U.S. Army Human Resources Command. N.d.

———. "Individual Deceased Personnel File: Charles Hulbert Suppes." U.S. Army Human Resources Command. N.d.

———. "Individual Deceased Personnel File: Ferguson Theodore Bell." U.S. Army Human Resources Command. N.d.

———. "Individual Deceased Personnel File: Jake Floyd Penick." U.S. Army Human Resources Command. N.d.

———. "Individual Deceased Personnel File: James Alfred Hinds." U.S. Army Human Resources Command. N.d.

———. "Individual Deceased Personnel File: Lee Vaughan Miller." U.S. Army Human Resources Command. N.d.

———. "Individual Deceased Personnel File: Leonard Harvey Phillips." U.S. Army Human Resources Command. N.d.

———. "Individual Deceased Personnel File: Lewis Marvin Shepard." U.S. Army Human Resources Command. N.d.

———. "Individual Deceased Personnel File: William Raymond Ronaghan." U.S. Army Human Resources Command. N.d.

Desert Training Center. "Blyth Army Airfield, California." https://deserttrainingcenter.com/blythe.html.

Edwards, Robert. *Aerial View of Bomber Mountain*. Photograph. N.d.

El Reno Athletics. "We Remember." https://www.elrenops.org/o/athletics/page/memorial-stadium-rededication.

El Reno Daily Tribune. "Cridermen Await Invasion of Classen Comets." October 27, 1936.

Bibliography

Encyclopædia Britannica. "Hi-Y Clubs." https://kids.britannica.com/students/article/Hi-Y-clubs/326403.
———. "Marshaling Yard." https://www.britannica.com/technology/marshaling-yard.
———. "*The Thousand and One Nights*." https://www.britannica.com/topic/The-Thousand-and-One-Nights.
Encyclopedia Dubuque. "American War Dads." State Historical Society of Iowa and the Iowa Museum Association. https://www.encyclopediadubuque.org/index.php/AMERICAN_WAR_DADS.
"Enlistment Record, New York Coast Guard." May 13, 1935. Ronaghan Family Collection, Jim Gatchell Memorial Museum.
Evening Courier. "Seeks to Identify 6 in West Plane Crash." August 13, 1945.
FBI. "What We Investigate." May 3, 2016. http://www.fbi.gov/investigate.
Find a Grave. "Helen Myers Newburn (1902–1996)." https://www.findagrave.com/memorial/26643012/helen-newburn.
———. "Iva L. Floyd Penick (1920–2014)." https://www.findagrave.com/memorial/125265269/iva-l-penick.
———. "2LT Anthony Joseph Tilotta (1919–1943)." https://www.findagrave.com/memorial/41572480/anthony-joseph-tilotta.
Florida Divorce Index. Lee, FL. 1937.
Forest Service. "Davy Crockett National Forest: National Forests and Grasslands in Texas." https://www.fs.usda.gov/detail/texas/about-forest/districts/?cid=fswdev3_008441.
447th Bomb Group. "42-31225 *Scheherazade*." https://447bg.com/fortresses-of-the-447th/42-31225.
Freeman, Roger A. *The B-17 Flying Fortress Story*. Arms and Armour Press, 1999.
"George Field Army Flying School." December 13, 1942. Ronaghan Family Collection, Jim Gatchell Memorial Museum.
Goolsby, Dana. "Winds of Change Leaves Waneta Community in the Dust of the Past." Waneta Community, Texas and School, Houston County. http://www.texasescapes.com/DanaGoolsby/Waneta-Community-and-School-Texas.htm.
GovInfo. "Archaeological Resources Protection Act of 1979 § (1979)." https://www.govinfo.gov/content/pkg/USCODE-2013-title16/html/USCODE-2013-title16-chap1B.htm.
Grubb, Kevin. Electronic correspondence with the author. March 2017.
Hamm, Kenneth G. Personal diary. 1945. Rock Springs Historical Museum Collection.
Hangar Thirteen. "Aircraft Camouflage." http://hangarthirteen.org/wp-content/uploads/2020/08/07-1-1-Aircraft-Camouflage.pdf.
Hinds, William. Email with the author. March 31, 2024.
———. Telephone interview with the author. April 25, 2020.

Bibliography

The Historical Marker Database. "Sioux Falls Army Technical School Historical Marker." April 1, 2021. https://www.hmdb.org/m.asp?m=169910.

Horwitz, Lewis I. Letter to Mary Ronaghan. August 31, 1945. Ronaghan Family Collection, Jim Gatchell Memorial Museum.

Jablonski, Edward. *Flying Fortress: The Illustrated Biography of the B-17s and the Men Who Flew Them.* Doubleday and Company, 1965.

John & Ann Gallentine. http://www.gallentine.org/.

Joseph F. Baugher. "1942 USAAF Serial Numbers (42-001 to 42-10959)." http://www.joebaugher.com/usaf_serials/1942_1.html.

Lexington Herald. "Bodies, Plane Found on Peak." August 13, 1945.

Linn, James. "Boeing B-17 Flying Fortress." The National World War II Museum. May 16, 2020. https://www.nationalww2museum.org/war/articles/boeing-b-17-flying-fortress.

Living New Deal. "Davy Crockett National Forest—Ratcliff TX." April 12, 2017. https://livingnewdeal.org/sites/davy-crockett-national-forest-ratcliff-tx/.

Maguire, Jon A. *Silver Wings, Pinks & Greens: Uniforms, Wings & Insignia of USAAF Airmen in World War II.* Atglen, PA: Schiffer Publishing, 1994.

Manhattan Beach News. "Sgt. James Hinds Found by Cowboys in Big Horn Mountains of Wyoming." August 28, 1945. Manhattan Beach Historical Society.

Marriage license. Big Horn County, MT. May 2, 1926.

———. Harris County, TX. July 17, 1941.

———. Hot Springs, WY. September 11, 1920.

Marriage Record no. 30. Comanche County, OK. August 2, 1941.

Massey, Irving. Letter to Forest Supervisor. December 10, 1945. Bighorn National Forest Historical Collection, Jim Gatchell Memorial Museum.

Maurer, Maurer. *Air Force Combat Units of World War II.* Chartwell Books, 1994.

———. *Combat Squadrons of the Air Force, World War II.* Albert F. Simpson Historical Research Center, 1982.

McAulay, Gary. Email with the author. April 3, 2024. Manhattan Beach Historical Society.

———. Email with the author. 2014. Manhattan Beach Historical Society.

Mentzinger, Francis J. Letter of Reference. January 11, 1937. Ronaghan Family Collection, Jim Gatchell Memorial Museum.

Miami News. "10 Bodies Removed from Lost Fortress." August 19, 1945.

Miller, Lee Vaughan. Letter to Wilson Miller. July 7, 1942. Miller Family Collection.

———. Letter to Wilson Miller. August 6, 1942. Miller Family Collection.

Missoulian. "Bodies Found High on Mountaintop." August 13, 1945.

The Montana Standard. "Plane Wreckage, Bodies Found." August 12, 1945.

Moore, Allen. "Little Jimmy Dickens Biography." PBS. https://www.pbs.org/kenburns/country-music/little-jimmy-dickens-biography.

Museum of Flight. "Boeing B-17F Flying Fortress: The Museum of Flight." https://www.museumofflight.org/exhibits-and-events/aircraft/boeing-b-17f-flying-fortress.
National Air and Space Museum. "Medal, American Campaign Medal." https://airandspace.si.edu/collection-objects/medal-american-campaign-medal/nasm_A19710124000.
National Archives and Records Administration. "Civilian Conservation Corps File: Jake Floyd Penick." N.d.
———. "Civilian Conservation Corps File: Lee Vaughan Miller." N.d.
National Historic Preservation Act of 1966, as Amended Through December 19, 2014, and Codified in Title 54 of the United States Code. https://www.rd.usda.gov/sites/default/files/NationalHistoricPreservationAct.pdf.
Newburn, Glenn E. Personal interview with the author. N.d.
O'Brien, William P. Letter to commanding general, Second Corps Area. October 1, 1941. Ronaghan Family Collection, Jim Gatchell Memorial Museum.
The Oriole. Evander Childs High School, 1936.
PBS. "Air War from 1939–1945: The Bombing of Germany." https://www.pbs.org/wgbh/americanexperience/features/bombing-air-war-1939-1945/.
Penick McDonald, Debra. Email with the author. February 9, 2015.
The Phoenician. Westmont-Upper Yoder High School, 1938.
Pilot Training Manual for the B-17 Flying Fortress. United States Army Air Force, n.d. http://303rdbg.com/crew-duties.html.
Raleigh Register. "Body of Glen Daniel Soldier Found After 2 Years' Entombment." August 19, 1945.
———. "Twenty-Seven Candidates at Trap Hill High." April 23, 1937.
Redondo Reflex. "Georgia Hinds in Yuma Wedding." May 4, 1950.
Rock Springs Daily Rocket-Miner. "Retired Judge Kenneth G. Hamm Dies." February 4, 1997.
Ronaghan Veale, Florence. Personal interview with the author. July 2009.
"Selective Service Registration: Charles Edgar Newburn." World War II Draft Registration Cards for Oklahoma, n.d.
"Selective Service Registration: Ferguson Theodore Bell." World War II Draft Registration Cards for Alabama, n.d.
"Selective Service Registration: James Alfred Hinds." World War II Draft Registration Cards for California, 1938.
Selma Times-Journal. "Lee Dunning Passes After Long Illness." January 18, 1945.
———. "Thomasville Flyer Plane Crash Victim." August 19, 1945.
Seminole Producer. "Flyers Identified Who Died in Crash Two Years Ago." August 19, 1945.
Shepard, Jack. Telephone interview with the author. October 16, 2014.
Shepard, Jack, and Pamela Shepard. Email with the author. January 28, 2015.

Bibliography

Shepard, Lewis Marvin. Letter to Leo Hazel Shepard. 1943. "Letters to Mother," Shepard Family Collection.

———. Letter to Leo Hazel Shepard. N.d. "Letters to Mother," Shepard Family Collection.

Shepard, Pamela. Telephone interview. Personal, January 28, 2015.

Sheridan Press. "Wreckage Found in Big Horns Called That of Army Airplane." August 15, 1945. Sheridan County Fulmer Public Library, The Wyoming Room.

Smithsonian National Air and Space Museum, Archives Division. "Individual Aircraft Record Card." July 8, 1943.

Stender, Walter W., and Evans Walker. "The National Personnel Records Center Fire: A Study in Disaster." *The American Archivist* 37, no. 4 (October 1974): 521–49. https://www.archives.gov/personnel-records-center/fire-1973.

Suppes, Betsy. Personal correspondence with the author. N.d.

Tilotta Family Collection. "Blackland Army Flying School." May 24, 1943.

Unidentified newspaper. "After 2 Years Snow Drift, Wister Boy Sent Home: Plane Wrecked on Snow Covered Slopes of Cloudy Peak, Wyoming, Near City Ten Sleep." 1945. Newburn Family Collection, Jim Gatchell Memorial Museum.

———. "Bluecoats Launch a Memorial." March 24, 1946. Ronaghan Family Collection, Jim Gatchell Memorial Museum.

———. "Body of Sgt. Jake Penick Found in Wyoming." 1945. Penick Family Collection, Jim Gatchell Memorial Museum.

———. "Bronx Airman Is Reported Missing." 1943. Ronaghan Family Collection, Jim Gatchell Memorial Museum.

———. "Crash Victim's Rites to Be Held in Jax." 1945. Shepard Family Collection.

———. "Mass Is Said for Safety of Missing Army Airman." N.d. Ronaghan Family Collection, Jim Gatchell Memorial Museum.

———. "Newest Police Patrol Boat Is Launched; Named for Lost Air Hero, Ex-Patrolman." N.d. Ronaghan Family Collection, Jim Gatchell Memorial Museum.

U.S. Army Air Corps. "Official Military Personnel File: Leonard Harvey Phillips." N.d.

U.S. Army Air Forces. "Description of Accident, Report of Aircraft Accident File." Historical Research Agency, Maxwell Air Force Base. August 1943.

U.S. Army Air Forces Technical School diploma. January 16, 1943. Shepard Family Collection.

U.S. Army Corps of Engineers. "Fort Myers Bombing and Gunnery Range." Formerly Used Defense Sites. https://www.saj.usace.army.mil/FortMyers/.

U.S. Census Bureau. Fifteenth census of the population, 1930. New York.

———. Fifteenth census of the population, 1930. Texas.

Bibliography

———. Fourteenth census of the population, 1920. Wyoming.

———. 1950 census. Wisconsin.

———. 1910 census. Pennsylvania.

———. Sixteenth census of the population, 1940. Alabama.

———. Sixteenth census of the population, 1940. Florida.

———. Sixteenth census of the population, 1940. Texas.

———. Twelfth census of the population, 1900. Pennsylvania.

U.S. Department of Defense. "Victory Over Japan Day: End of WWII." https://www.defense.gov/Multimedia/Experience/VJ-Day/#banner.

U.S. Naturalization Service. "Petition for Naturalization." January 1, 1940.

Valentine, Lewis J. Letter to Mary Ronaghan. November 20, 1944. Ronaghan Family Collection, Jim Gatchell Memorial Museum.

Van Nest, John D. Letter to William B. Fay. February 5, 1946. Bighorn National Forest Historical Collection, Jim Gatchell Memorial Museum.

Veale, Jim. "Babe." *The Sentry* 21, no. 4 (October 2012): 5–7.

———. Email with the author. April 30, 2024.

———. Email with the author. May 20, 2024.

Wendover Aerial Gunnery School. n.d. Photograph. Jim Gatchell Memorial Museum.

Western Union Telegram. August 18, 1945. Shepard Family Collection.

———. August 19, 1945. Shepard Family Collection.

Westmont Presbyterian Church. Dedication of the Charles Hulbert Suppes III Memorial Chapel. Johnstown, PA. 1946.

Wiberg, Eric. "62 Sail and Steam Cargo Vessels from Bahamas 1957, from Mercantile Navy List & Maritime Directory." March 7, 2017. https://ericwiberg.com/2013/07/62-sail-and-steam-cargo-vessels-from-bahamas-1957-from-mercantile-navy-list-maritime-directory.

Wichita Falls Times. "Bodies Recovered After 25 Months." August 19, 1945.

Wolfenbarger, Vesta. Letter to Berl Bader. September 12, 1945. Bader Family Collection.

World War II Veterans' Compensation Bureau. "Application for World War II Compensation." Commonwealth of Pennsylvania. January 11, 1951.

Wyoming State Tribune. "Fisher Rites Will Be Held Here Thursday." January 15, 1941. Wyoming State Archives.

Yearbook. Williamson Free School of Mechanical Trades, 1917.

Yenne, Bill. *Building the B-17 Flying Fortress: A Detailed Look at Manufacturing Boeing's Legendary World War II Bomber in Original Photos.* Specialty Press, 2020.

INDEX

A

aircraft lost 15
American Legion
  Post 184, Redondo Beach, California 36
  Thomasville, Alabama Post 40
American War Dads Association 114, 115, 118, 121, 122, 126

B

Bader, Berl 77, 105–110
ball turret 49
Baraboo, Wisconsin 39
Beckley, West Virginia 44, 45, 47
Bell, Ferguson Theodore 37–41, 115, 121
Bomber Mountain 13, 59, 127, 132, 136
  naming 114, 126
Bronx, New York 18, 72, 74, 75, 92, 113, 132
Buffalo, Wyoming 40, 59, 76, 95, 103, 107, 113, 120, 129, 132

C

Casper, Wyoming 26, 39, 40, 41, 67, 76, 79, 114, 128, 129, 130
Civilian Conservation Corps 42, 44, 45, 51, 52, 115
Clayton, Kansas 27
Cloud Peak 13, 40, 79, 81, 101, 108, 109, 112, 118, 120, 127
Cloud Peak Wilderness 13, 132, 136

D

Dickens, James Cecil 44
Douglas Aircraft Company 15, 16, 34, 131

E

El Reno, Oklahoma 34, 35

INDEX

F

Florence Lake 81, 99, 102, 103, 114, 118, 120, 126, 137
Fort Sill, Oklahoma 52

G

Grand Island, Nebraska 16, 17, 22, 27, 35, 39, 45, 67, 68, 72, 73, 76, 92, 101, 112, 119, 128

H

Hamm, Kenneth 79, 81, 87, 92, 93–104, 107
Hermosa Beach, California 34, 35, 109
Hinds, James Alfred 34–36, 45, 109, 115, 120, 140
Horton, William 79, 95, 102, 103
Houston, Texas 23, 24, 25, 51

J

Jacksonville, Florida 54, 58, 120
Johnstown, Pennsylvania 31, 32

L

Lewis, William 81, 87, 94, 95, 97, 102, 103, 106, 107, 108, 120
Lieutenant Ronaghan No. 1 22, 113
Long Beach, California 15, 16, 34, 131
Love Field, Texas 16

M

machine gun 39
Manhattan Beach, California 36

Massey, Irving 78, 81, 99, 102, 109, 118, 120, 122, 123, 126
McRae, George 81, 102, 103
Miller, Lee Vaughan 42–47, 115, 121
Mistymoon Lake 119, 136

N

Newburn, Charles Edgar 48–50, 107, 108, 115, 121

O

Obert, Charles 79, 95, 103
Omaha, Nebraska 26

P

Pendleton, Oregon 16, 17, 20, 22, 35, 39, 45, 67, 68, 72, 73, 76, 92, 101, 112, 119
Penick, Jake Floyd 51–53, 115, 121
Phillips, Leonard Harvey 26–30, 68, 70, 72, 73, 111, 112, 115, 121, 130, 132
Plummer Provisional Group 16, 17, 119
Post, Urban 81, 120, 126

R

Rapid City
  Army Air Base 40, 79, 81, 92, 93, 97, 106, 112, 119, 120
  South Dakota 39, 40, 87, 92
Riverton, Wyoming 37, 38, 105
Rock Springs, Wyoming 27, 93
Ronaghan, William Raymond 16, 18–22, 67, 68, 72, 74, 75, 76, 92, 112, 113, 115, 121, 126, 129, 130, 132

S

Scharazad 13, 15, 16, 17, 32, 57, 67, 76, 77, 132
Scheherazade
  B-17G 14
  origin 14
Shepard, Lewis Marvin 16, 54–66, 115, 120
Sheridan, Wyoming 39, 40, 76, 114, 115, 118, 121, 122, 123, 126, 127
Shoshoni, Wyoming 37
Suppes, Charles Hulbert 13, 14, 31–33, 115, 120
Surveyor, West Virginia 42

T

tail gun 55
Thomasville, Alabama 37, 38, 40, 41
Tilotta, Anthony Joseph 23–25, 35, 115, 121
top gun turret 36, 118

W

waist gun 53
Walla Walla, Washington 16, 17, 30, 57, 65, 72, 74
Waneta, Oklahoma 51
weather 67, 76, 112
Wister, Oklahoma 48, 50, 108, 121

ABOUT THE AUTHOR

Sylvia A. Bruner has worked in the museum field since 2000. As the executive director of the Jim Gatchell Memorial Museum, she has guided the museum through reaccreditation with the American Alliance of Museums and receiving the Institute for Museum and Library Services' National Medal. The museum is the repository of artifacts relating to Bomber Mountain and has a permanent exhibit on the topic, offering Bruner a constant reminder to research and compile this story. Along with being an active volunteer in various history and community organizations, Bruner enjoys spending time horseback riding and camping with her family in the Bighorn Mountains.